Y0-DKO-558

It's Just COMMON-SENSE

60 WISE HELPS FROM
PROVERBS TO GUIDE
YOUR EVERYDAY
DECISIONS

Florence Simmons

Pleasant Word
A Division of WINEPRESS PUBLISHING

© 2006 by Florence Simmons. All rights reserved.

Printed in the United States of America

Packaged by Pleasant Word, a division of WinePress Publishing, PO Box 428, Enumclaw, WA 98022. The views expressed or implied in this work do not necessarily reflect those of Pleasant Word, a division of WinePress Publishing. Ultimate design, content, and editorial accuracy of this work are the responsibilities of the author.

No part of this publication may be reproduced, stored in a retrieval system, or transmitted in any way by any means—electronic, mechanical, photocopy, recording, or otherwise—without the prior permission of the copyright holder, except as provided by USA copyright law.

Unless otherwise noted, all Scriptures are taken from the Holy Bible, New International Version, Copyright © 1973, 1978, 1984 by the International Bible Society. Used by permission of Zondervan Publishing House. The "NIV" and "New International Version" trademarks are registered in the United States Patent and Trademark Office by International Bible Society.

Scripture references marked RSV are taken from the Revised Standard Version of the Bible, copyright 1952 [2nd edition, 1971] by the Division of Christian Education of the National Council of the Churches of Christ in the United States of America. Used by permission. All rights reserved.

Scripture references marked KJV are taken from the King James Version of the Bible.

Scripture references marked NASB are taken from the New American Standard Bible, © 1960, 1963, 1968, 1971, 1972, 1973, 1975, 1977 by The Lockman Foundation. Used by permission.

ISBN 1-4141-0197-X
Library of Congress Catalog Card Number: 2004093404

I dedicate this devotional to my
supportive family:
Husband David, Daughter and Son-in-law Cheryl and Steve,
Grandchildren Sarah, Rachael, Ross
Daughters and Sons-in-law Carol and Mark,
Caren and Troy

Table of Contents

Introduction 9

Start Right 10
Who Is Being Influenced? 12
Reject Wisdom? 14
Blessings Await You 16
Bind Them in the Heart 18
Trust and Acknowledge 20
I'm Too Smart 22
Bless His Work 24
Don't Despise Discipline 26
Beginning to the End 28
Preserve Sound Judgment 30
Taken for Granted 32
Pick a Side 34
Listen and Heed 36
Guard Your Heart 38
What Did You Say? 40
The Path 42
You're Being Watched 44
Ensnared 46
Ant or Sluggard 48
Arrogance 50
Wicked Scheming 52

Affairs 54
Long for and Seek it 56
A-t-t-i-t-u-d-e 58
Wise Father, Wise Son 60
Memory of the Righteous 62
Take Advice 64
H-a-t-r-e-d 66
Have You Heard . . . ? 68
Willing to Be Instructed 70
Humility Allows Wisdom 72
I-n-t-e-g-r-i-t-y 74
Have Righteous Leaders 76
Deceptive Wages 78
The Wise Win Souls 80
Words That Hurt or Heal 82
Are You Anxious or Happy? 84
Store Up the Word 86
A Truthful Witness 88
Hot, Hot! 90
Discontentment Is Costly 92
Prayers of the Upright 94
Corrupted by a Bribe 96
My Plans or His Plans? 98
Conflict in the Home 100
His Name, a Strong Tower 102
The Blame Game 104
Payback 106
Strength & Splendor! 108
God Is in Control 110
Getting Weary to Get Wealthy? 112
Don't Envy Sinners 114
Rise Up—Again 116
Don't Gloat 118
A Fitting Word 120
Do You Have a Tomorrow? 122
The Gap 124
Speak Up 126
The Super Woman 128

The fear of the Lord is the beginning of wisdom, and knowledge of the Holy One is understanding.

—*Proverbs 9:10*

Introduction

Common sense wisdom is desperately needed in our topsy-turvy world today because common sense isn't very common any more. Welcome to "It's Just Common-Sense," the words of wisdom to help you live more successfully in your world today.

A person has common sense wisdom when they make sensible judgments, and when they know how to skillfully and rightfully judge life's situations so they will respond to them in a wise way. Therefore, God's Word encourages us to get wisdom, knowledge and understanding to help us to live in a manner pleasing to God so that we will not be unwise in our decisions, actions or speech.

These devotions speak to such topics as envy, strife, discipline, wealth, affairs, pride, hatred, gossip, or having an anxious heart, all key issues we encounter every day. Sometimes there is only one scripture that deals with a topic at the beginning of the devotion—other times several scriptures will be included which will enhance your understanding. At the end of the devotion is a prayer to help confirm what the devotion encourages you to do.

As you read the devotion with an *open* mind and heart you will receive the Word that God's Spirit desires just for you.

Start Right

The fear of the Lord is the beginning of knowledge.

—Proverbs 1:7
(Read also: Proverbs 2:1–5, 9:10)

Solomon, the third king of Israel, was overwhelmed when he took his place as king after his father, King David, died. In a dream God appeared to Solomon saying, "Ask for whatever you want me to give you" (1 Kings 3:5). Solomon replied, "Give me wisdom and knowledge, that I may lead this people" (1 Kings 3:9). *He made* a very *wise* request. Solomon realized he was not able to lead the people in his own strength and ability.

The New Testament tells us that one greater than Solomon is here. That is Jesus Christ, the Son of God, "one who has become for us wisdom from God" (1 Corinthians 1:30). Solomon's revelation was that the "fear of the Lord is the beginning of wisdom," and "of knowledge" (Proverbs 9:10, 1:7). *What exactly is the "fear of the Lord"?* Let's take a look at one main aspect of the fear of the Lord.

The prophet Isaiah once had a vision in which he found himself in the presence of the Almighty God. All heaven was responding to God with worship—God's glory and holiness so affected Isaiah that he responded, "Woe is me! I am ruined! For I am a man of unclean lips, . . . and my eyes have seen the King, the Lord Almighty" (Isaiah 6:5). In this holy presence Isaiah stood in overwhelming reverential *awe* and *fear*, aware of *his own imperfections* and his impure *spiritual qualifications* before the mighty Maker of the universe.

True wisdom begins to develop in us when we too have this holy "awe and fear." We gain understanding when we verbally acknowledge to God that without Him we too are desperately spiritually bankrupted. Along with this reverential awe should come a holy fear of sinning against Him and His revealed Word. Our desire then is to actively and passionately determine to please Him and be in obedience to *His will, not our will.*

The wise then are those who personally and fervently desire to experience God, receive His wisdom and obey *His* laws for their lives. It's just that simple. This wisdom is available to *every* single one who seeks it. The Bible says, "If *any* of you lack wisdom, he should ask God, who gives generously to *all* without finding fault, and it will be given to him" (James 1:5).

When you apply the wisdom from God's Word and spend quality time in His presence you can make right decisions for your life. Seeking God will guarantee help with raising your family, will direct you in right relationships, and will guide you away from making foolish choices. Like Solomon, we can start right with the beginning of wisdom—the *"fear of the Lord."*

Prayer: Almighty God, as Isaiah, I am one of unclean lips aware of my own imperfection and spiritual failings. I recognize the necessity for Your "awe" and wisdom in my life. Produce in me a holy fear of sinning against You and Your Holy Word. In Jesus name, amen.

Unwise actions: Fools reject the "fear of the Lord."

Who Is Being Influenced?

My son, if sinners entice you do not give into them . . . do not go with them, do not set foot on their paths.

—Proverbs 1:10,15
(Read also: Proverbs 2:11–15, 4:14–16)

*P*owerful and provocative advice is given by Solomon to his son—don't run with any crowd of sinners who want to entice you into doing wrong. There are some very wicked people in this world—those who serve *your enemy*, who are determined to kill, steal, and destroy your life, spiritually and physically. They may appear to be very cordial people, but they are shrewdly able to persuade anyone. The Bible says that the enemy comes in sheep's clothing (Matthew 7:15).

We need wisdom to see the disguise they wear, so "Wisdom will save you from the ways of the wicked men." Solomon declares, and "He who walks with the wise grows wise, but a companion of fools suffers harm" (Proverbs 2:11–15, 13:20). Fools are those who follow the crowd; the wise patiently deal with their critical wisecracks knowing rightly what constitutes a fool, those who deny God's Word and wisdom. Their values are disagreeable to Him and committed believers.

A celebrity on television recently said that 10 percent of the population are ingesting drugs and "I was one of them". Someone introduced him to drugs and in time he became addicted to cocaine. He was losing everything. His family gave him an ultimatum of changing or being rejected by them all. He was in a dilemma. His habit was well entrenched. Lack of God's wisdom led him astray, and foolishly he almost lost everything.

Jet speedily away from the world's temptations: evil friends, alcohol, dishonest business deals, the enticement of pornography, etc. If you are involved in any of these debaucheries, get out now.

The apostle Paul warns us, "Do not be yoked together with unbelievers. For what do righteousness and wickedness have in common? Or what fellowship can light have with darkness?" (2 Corinthians 6:14).

This world delights when we conform to their standards. Believers are here to shine as a beacon among the darkness of its sinful ways. We can't demonstrate Christ if we partake in their wickedness. The Word calls us to be separate (2 Corinthians 6:17). Yes, we reside in this world, but we are to resist conforming to its untamed passions and sinful nature. Jesus explains, "You do not belong to the world, but I have chosen you out of the world. That is why the world hates you" (John 15:19b).

Craving a deeper spiritual walk gives one the tenacity to be a *positive, Christlike influence*. Power-packed Christian living will strengthen you to shun the values of the wicked and access you powerful strength to deny acting with them. Impact others for Christ around you. Reject any corrupt influence that determines to destroy you. Let your spiritual influence and godly life speak to your own world. Influence them for Christ.

Prayer: Lord I desire to be a positive influence for You in my world. Responding from Your wisdom and power, I can accomplish this. I open myself to receive from You. Thank You, in Jesus name, amen.

Unwise actions: Being enticed by fools to sinful escapades.

Reject Wisdom?

> Wisdom calls aloud . . . since you rejected me when I called . . . I in turn will laugh at your disaster.
>
> —Proverbs 1: 20,24,26
> (Read also: Proverbs 3:22–23, 8:36)

The security camera caught the man who entered the mall store after closing.

With a rediculous solid sack over his head to conceal his identity, he stumbled around in the store. He exited the back door returning after he ripped holes in the sack for his eyes, and with a flashlight began to help himself to the merchandise. The police apprehended him speedily when the surveillance camera identified him as the mall security guard. How could they tell? He still had his security guard uniform on!

The consequences of his brainless decision to attempt this burglary were: losing his job, his credibility, his integrity, trust from others, and possibly even his freedom. He did it for greed but gained painful regret. Solomon says, "Wisdom is too high for a fool" (Proverbs 24:7). P. T. Barnum, the originator of the Barnum Bailey Circus said, "There's a fool born every minute." Fools, those who reject wisdom, have been known to:

> Reject good advice and accept regretful advice, flatten their paycheck on booze, leaving zilch for their family needs, blow their earnings on slot machines, believe what belongs to others is theirs (and they

steal to get it), expound that the world owes them a living, and the list goes on.

Did you ever wonder why certain people you know can never seem to "get it together"? Everything they seem to do negatively boomerangs on them. Their life is static, going nowhere; they can't stay at a job, their families are suffering, and their finances are in shambles. Somewhere along their life's journey, wisdom called out to help them through a friend, a neighbor, a teacher, or a relative. For various reasons they were not willing to receive the wisdom offered to them from these interested individuals. Maybe they didn't have enough positive role models or, as they aged, bitterness set in their hearts blinding them. It could be they rejected wise helpful advice and *chose* to hang with the hordes of this world.

Seekers of wisdom will grab hold of this warning, "There is a way that seems right to a man, but *in the end it leads to death*" (Proverbs 16:25). Clamp on to this advice, "Whoever fails to find me (wisdom) harms himself" (Proverbs 8:36). Our past may sometimes hinder us, but as *we earnestly seek Jesus Christ with an open heart*, He who has all wisdom will reveal it to us.

Why would anyone in their right mind reject God's wisdom? They may not be willing to commit their mind to be transformed through God's Word. Your *willingness* to receive is essential. Remember, wisdom "will prolong your life many years and bring you prosperity" (Proverbs 3:2). Don't reject His wisdom.

Prayer: Father, I have allowed hindrances in the past to distract me from receiving the wisdom I need so desperately. I have been a fool in many ways. Grant me Your wisdom in every situation of my life. Thank You, in Jesus name, amen.

Unwise thoughts: I can do it my way on my own.

Blessings Await You

He holds victory in store for the upright, he is a shield to those whose walk is blameless, for he guards the course of the just and protects the way of his faithful ones.

—Proverbs 2:7–8
(Read also: 11:20; Psalm 84:11)

*I*t is fantastic to be blessed! Has anyone ever blessed you? A friend may have extended to you an invitation to a wonderful meal, or a believer noticed your need and supplied it. Blessings come when a deliverer shovels our snow, rakes our lawn, or take us out for coffee or a Coke. To be blessed makes one feel very exceptional.

Countless blessings await a believer who is earnestly seeking to gain wisdom. God delights when His children choose to worship Him, seek His fellowship, and desire His direction for their daily battles. When we determine to walk in the "fear of the Lord," "He has counsel in store for the upright, He is the shield of those who walk honestly." As Protector and Counselor He stands available (Proverbs 2:7 NAB).

Your enemies may bring accusations against you; the Lord Almighty will be your shield of *protection*. The stride of the upright need not fear any of mankind's cunning designs. Ask the Lord for right *counsel* for any situation—work problems, raising kids, stressed family relationships, or spiritual direction.

With *wisdom* and *understanding* you will be blessed to discern good from evil, avoiding the pitfalls of off-beam choices that can attribute to a disastrous life. The Holy Spirit can accomplish this as He works to bring your desires in line with the Father's, so that God's commandments and ways become your requests. The Psalmist spoke this way, "Your commandments fill me with delight, I love them deeply" (Psalm 119:47, Jerusalem Bible). When we delight in His life's instructions for us with a sincere inward longing, we will be re-energized and trained to discern God's way from the world's wickedness—valuable knowledge to possess.

Wisdom enables us to choose decent and upright friends. When wisdom operates in us, we will sense and know those whose hearts are spiritually attuned with God's Word and have a desire to serve Him. Righteous friends are a blessing to us. The Psalmist was an honorable friend. "I am a friend to all who fear you, to all who follow your precepts," he exclaims (Psalm 119:63).

This following translation assures, "Keeping good and upright companions will preserve thee from the evil way. From the man that speaks perverseness" (Proverbs 2:12 ABPS). You will be kept on a blessed path, "So that you may go in the way of good men, and keep in the footsteps of the upright" (Proverbs 2:20 BAS).

Rely on the 7,000 promises and blessings that await you as you resolutely grasp wisdom for today. Seek to intake them with an open heart from your heavenly Father.

Prayer: Yes, Father, I bow in reverence to You and open my heart to receive all that You have for me today. Thank You for Your past and present blessings and also my future ones as I actively keep Your Word. In Jesus name, amen.

Unwise actions: Closing your heart, abandoning His blessings.

Bind Them in the Heart

Let love and faithfulness never leave you; bind them around your neck; write them on the tablet of your heart.

—Proverbs 3:3
(Read also: Proverbs 6:20–23)

Jewelry catalogs, stores, and gift shops carry an array of beautiful crosses. They can be pinned on, worn as necklaces, and even worn on rings. Wearing a cross is an instant tribute of Christ's sacrifice for us.

The Jews were commanded to keep certain yearly rituals as remembrances of what God had done for them. One commemoration was their catastrophic experience when they were delivered from slavery in Egypt by the mighty hand of God. They were to observe this experience, known as the Passover, for seven days every year. Moses informed them, "This observance will be for you like a sign on your hand and a reminder on your forehead that the law of the Lord is to be on your lips" (Exodus 13:9).

The Jews then, literally, made two small leather boxes, which they attached in such a way that they could wear one on the forehead and one on the arm. These contained vellum on which would be written portions of the Mosaic Law. As they repeated the Law written, it enforced appreciation and acknowledgement of God's acts and mighty power in delivering them.

Moses reminded the people after their deliverance, to "Love the Lord your God with all your heart and with all your soul and with all your strength. These commandments that I give you today are to be upon your hearts" (Deuteronomy 6:5). Their small boxes, or our crosses today, are heart symbols that God's Word should be on *our* lips.

Love and faithfulness to the Lord and His written Word is an integral part of a believer's life. It is of great importance to have God's Word hidden in our heart. The Word will literally direct us in life's difficult decisions and keep us from sinning against our heavenly Father. The Psalmist realized this importance and wrote, "I have hidden *your word in my heart* that *I might not sin against you*" (Psalm 119:11).

You may wail, "I have so many *things* going on today in my life. How can I have this constant remembrance of the Word in my heart at all times?" Here are a few suggestions: write or print scripture on paper. Tape it up before your eyes on your refrigerator, bathroom mirror, desk, or dashboard of your car. Associate word pictures to help you, such as Psalm 89:13, "Your arm is endued with power, your hand is strong"—i.e., arm, power, hand, strong. *Meditate* on its meaning in the shower, driving, or walking; *repeat* and memorize it. That's what it means to "hide" it in your heart. The Lord will then bring these scriptures to your remembrance as help when situations arise.

"Let love and faithfulness never leave you, write them on the tablet of your heart." Start memorizing today.

Prayer: Lord, I've never been very good at memorizing, but I do want to hide Your Word in my heart. I ask for Your help to do that. In Jesus name, amen.

Unwise words: I can't memorize them.

Trust and Acknowledge

Trust in the Lord with all your heart and lean not on your own understanding; in all your ways acknowledge him, and he will make your paths straight.

—Proverbs 3:5–6
(Read also: Proverbs 28:26)

*T*rust. What does that mean to you? Can you trust most people's word today? Just whom can we believe or trust? The consumer is often lied to, or told half-truths, to convince them to buy a product. Information on the news is frequently given a one-sided twist making us speculate on the whole issue. Then another source gives us additional information, and we conclude we've been misled.

Trust is important to understanding God's Word. If we judge it according to the world's standards, we might say it can't be trusted. But God's Word is *above* and *beyond* the world's standards of trust. The Hebrew word for trust "batah" means—to confide in, so as to be *secure without fear*. We necessitate this kind of "secure without fear" trust in our lives today. That trust can only be realized when a believer maintains a strong committed relationship with Christ. These dedicated occasions teach His Word is truthful and dependable. Use of deception can never be attributed to God.

Every day we make decisions. Some are fairly easy, like what should I have for supper tonight? Other decisions demand much more thought—and prayer. When we trust in Christ, we will not "lean on our own understanding," but will "acknowledge Him in all our ways." Why? Because when *we do*, He will direct our paths. Then our *insignificant* or *demanding* decisions will be according to *His* plan.

It took trust and obedience for *Noah* to build an ark when God told him He was going to release a flood upon the earth. For Noah to picture a flood was unequal to what he could understand. He never saw rain from heaven or a flood before, *but* he believed and trusted what he had heard from God (Genesis 6:14–22).

Abraham left his family and stepped out on God's Word. "The Lord had said to Abram, (God changed his name to Abraham later) "Leave your country, your people . . . go to the land I will show you. I will make you into a great nation" (Genesis 12:1–2). God knew what lessons of discipleship would make Abraham the father of a great nation, but Abraham didn't.

Trust sometimes means walking by faith. Are you perplexed or questioning a decision? Is Christ asking you to trust Him? Our own understanding is limited and subject to error. *His directions lead us into His perfect will.* You can be assured that your heavenly Father, who loves you, will care for you, guiding you in every event according to *His purpose for you.* Trust Him, lean on Him, acknowledge Him and He will direct all your paths. Start that journey today.

Prayer: Heavenly Father, I'm hindered at times to know how to trust You. My focus seems only on how I *can solve* my own problems. I acknowledge that I desperately need You to direct my paths according to Your purpose for my life. In Jesus name, amen.

Unwise actions: Leaning on your own understanding.

I'm Too Smart

Do not be wise in your own eyes; fear the Lord and shun evil.
—Proverbs 3:7
(Read also: 3:8, 14:12, 28:26)

*E*ric had been cleverly concealing his recurrent stealing from the company where he was employed. He reminded himself, "I'm too smart and cunning to be caught. I'm extremely careful, and I protect myself." To Eric, he was wise in his own eyes. Proverbs 15:10 cautions us, "Stern discipline awaits him who leaves the path" Eventually Eric's cleverness was outwitted. He encountered a termination of his job, a soiled reputation, and paid heavy consequences for his deceit.

Occasionally I stroll by a calm lake in the evening. I take extreme pleasure in the radiance of the multi-colors from the sun's reflections in the water. Reflection is described powerfully in Proverbs 15:10. "As water reflects a face, so a man's heart reflects the man." It is unwise to embrace a self-centered ego; it is arrogance, *which mirrors what really is in your heart.* Trusting in "self" *never* places us in the right position to solve our problems.

"Do not be wise in your own *conceit*" is one translation of verse 7 (Septuagint). Conceit *proudly* displays ones marvelous abilities, amazing looks or the abundant talents *one* possess, but not *God's power in us.* These characteristics involve our carnal nature and lead to man's stumbling ways, not God's path.

When we "fear the Lord," we literally bring right direction to our spiritual being. No longer will we *crave* to walk in our own wisdom. As we hungrily partake of God's Word, we fill ourselves up with righteous longings. This hunger makes us realize that without God's Holy Spirit working in us we rightly have *no* abilities, talents, wisdom or understanding of our own. Our enlightened minds recognize that *all we receive* is from our heavenly Father.

The values and pressures of our shrewd world demand we depend on material ways to satisfy us, and our society requires increased worldly involvement and less family life. We find ourselves weighed down by these expectations; in turn, these pressures affect us physically, creating aches and pains of all kinds. When we "fear the Lord and shun evil," we have a promise in verse 8, "This will bring health to your body and nourishment to your bones." That sounds like a good offer to me.

Jesus does avail to you peace in the middle of any troubling situation, work problems, health dilemma, raising children, spouse compatibility and more. You don't have to lean on being "wise in your own eyes," but *lean on His wisdom*, which is far *greater than* any earthly wisdom. Proverbs 28:26 acknowledges it this way: "He who trusts in himself is a fool, but he who walks in wisdom is kept safe." Be farsighted; don't be smart in your own wisdom—seek His.

Prayer: Lord, I have looked more to earthly wisdom than I have looked to Your wisdom. It has not brought me the help and satisfaction I desired. As I seek Your wisdom, I invite Your Spirit to merge my heart with Your heart. In Jesus name, amen.

Unwise thoughts: I am so smart and clever.

Bless His Work

Honor the Lord with your wealth, with the firstfruits of all your crops.

—Proverbs 3:9
(Read also: 3:10, 11:25, Romans 12:8)

A businessman had an up and coming moving equipment company. He was also a Christian, and as president he could handle the profits in his own way. At the beginning he tithed 10 percent of his income and saw his profits increase. He began to see needs for financial help in missions and other areas so he expanded his giving to 20 percent of his profit. Over time, he increased his giving when he realized that he was being blessed so he could be a partner in God's work and kingdom. Toward the end of his life, he was giving 90 percent of his profits to God.

We in America are blessed in many ways. You might respond, "I'm not," but when you actually take account of your full cupboards, your full closets, a warm home, and cars, you will realize *you are* blessed compared to a majority of the world's population. God simply asks of us to give our tithe, 10 percent of our income plus offerings, from what *He has allowed us to earn.* Give it into the storehouse where you are spiritually fed. This is our *first priority.* When we take this step in obedience to God's Word, we will find no lack in our own needs. We are to honor the Lord with our *firstfruits,* the first part of our earnings. This principle *really* works.

It is true that certain people have much more wealth than others. God has entrusted many with added wealth to graciously and generously provide for His kingdom. Don't make the mistake that if God blesses you with added resources you should purchase a bigger house, more playthings, or more cars. No—that's not what it's all about. We are allowed additional wealth for a purpose—so we can be His arm to bless *His work*.

We will all have to give an account to God someday of how we used the position and wealth He delegated to us. The apostle John reminds us that we show God's love, this way. "If anyone has material possessions and sees his brother in need but has no pity on him, how can the love of God be in him? Let us not love with words or tongue but with actions and in truth" (1 John 3:17–18).

Your mailbox might hold urgent requests for needs. These wants can range from *foreign mission* needs—food, clothing, churches destroyed, *home mission* needs—helping to start a new church or requests, right in your local church and community. If God has entrusted you with added wealth show God's love with truthful "actions." His call to you is to give more abundantly to His kingdom. Honor Him with your means and bless His work.

Prayer: Thank You Father, for giving me financial blessings. Let me remember that I have been entrusted with them for Your work. I will be obedient to give back to You from the abundance You have delegated to me. In Jesus name, amen.

Unwise actions: Withholding when I have the power to give.

Don't Despise Discipline

Do not despise the Lord's discipline and do not resent his rebuke, because the Lord disciplines those he loves.
—Proverbs 3:11–12 (Read also: 15:31)

*T*he phrase, "This hurts me more than it does you" was never heard in my home as a child. Mom was the enforcer of discipline, and there were times I definitely knew I deserved it. Now as an adult, I realize how vital correction was for me. Discipline is "training that develops into self-control." An unconcerned mother and father would have made me unqualified for real life circumstances and assured my failure. When parent's love and care for their children, they cleave out a way for them to live and survive in this hectic world.

Believers become trained through God's Word and life experiences. In God's mercy and endless love for us, He at times sends discipline to direct us into His will. God's purpose for the Israelites was that they become a holy people and honor Him. They were to be separate from the wicked nations around them. He desired to lead them, fight for them, and direct them. As long as they held fast to His laws they were blessed with His presence and power.

The prophet Isaiah gives us a description of the Israelites attitude during his time. "They have forsaken the Lord; they have spurned the Holy One of Israel and turned their backs on Him" (Isaiah 1:4). The Israelites had *accepted* the corrupt and immoral ways of the heathen nations, living in wickedness and worshipping their gods. Through

His prophet Isaiah, God continues to call them back to Him, and they continually reject Him. God finally uses the Assyrians as "the rod of mine anger" to "seize loot and snatch plunder, and to trample them down" (Isaiah 10:5–6).

We may not notice the downward slide in *our* spiritual position. It concerns the Lord. He observes our wayward path and our involvement in the crookedness of this world. Like the Israelites He continues to call us back to Him, allowing situations in our lives that compel us to assess our withdrawn actions from Him: an accident, a physical need, and a impossible situation that only He can change. (Not all difficulties in our lives are solely for this purpose.) Solomon gives this advice, "He who ignores discipline despises himself, but whoever heeds corrections gains understanding" (Proverbs 14:32).

The apostle Paul shares profound thoughts to the Corinthians, and us. "When we are judged by the Lord, we are being disciplined so that we will *not* be condemned with the world" (1 Corinthians 11:32). We don't want to become stiff-necked and obstinate like the Israelites. Let's avidly strive to become strengthened in our faith by *walking in obedience* and *acting on* His Word. Earnestly seeking God daily will keep our ears attuned and our hearts open to Him.

Don't despise discipline, but learn that "He who listens to a life-giving rebuke will be at home among the wise" (Proverbs 15:31).

Prayer: Thank You, Father, for Your loving care and for drawing me to You through discipline. Continue to conform me to Your will for my life. In Jesus name, amen.

Unwise actions: Rebelling against God's discipline.

Beginning to the End

By wisdom the Lord laid the earth's foundations, by understanding he set the heavens in place.

—Proverbs 3:19
(Read also: Proverbs 8:22–31)

*Q*uestions. Questions. Excited and curious four-year-old Katie inquired, "Mommy, who makes the birds?" The mother replied, "God does." "Who made the flowers?" Katie questioned. Her mom explained to her that God made all things. Later that day the mother noticed Katie's toy strewn room and exclaimed, "Who made this mess?" Without hesitation Katie replied, "God."

Like Katie, many of us also have unanswered questions. One uncertainty we want to know is what wisdom brought about the world's formation? The logic of many on this issue has been finely debated for ages. Solomon knew nothing about the Big Bang theory some 3,000 years ago when he penned the above scripture.

Three hundred years later, Jeremiah, the prophet under the inspiration of God, acknowledged, "God made the world by his *power*, he founded the world *by his wisdom* and stretched out the heavens by his *understanding*" (Jeremiah 10:12). Both of these men believed and accepted the message they received—that by God's wisdom and understanding the heavens and earth were set in place. Psalm 93:2 instructs us, "Your throne (Lord) was established long ago; you are from all eternity.

Seven hundred years before Christ was born, Isaiah the prophet foretold of Christ: "The Spirit of the Lord will rest on him—the Spirit of *wisdom* and of *understanding*, the Spirit of counsel and of power, the Spirit of *knowledge* and of the fear of the Lord" (Isaiah 11:2). The apostle Paul tells the Colossians that in Christ "are hidden all the treasures of wisdom and knowledge" (Colossians 2:3). Isaiah's prophecy was affirmed when Jesus, God's Son, with Him from the beginning, came to earth and demonstrated this wisdom and understanding, then powerfully defeated sin on the cross for us.

Accept these truths: (1) God's wisdom, power and understanding were there at the beginning of creation. (2) Jesus, God's Son, was also with Him, and became for us the embodiment of the Spirit of wisdom, understanding, and knowledge.

Hebrews 1:3 informs us, "After Jesus provided purification for sin, he sat down at the right hand of the Majesty in heaven." Jesus is at the right hand of His Father, making intercession for every believer. The apostle Paul interceded for those in Colosse that God would "*fill you* with the knowledge of his will through all spiritual *wisdom* and *understanding.*" The reason: "that you may *live a life worthy of the Lord* and may please him in every way: *bearing fruit* in every good work, growing in the knowledge of God" (Colossians 1:10–11). Receive for yourself this powerful prayer for wisdom and understanding.

From the *beginning to the end* of the world, God remains the source of all wisdom. God's Word proclaims He hasn't changed; He "is the same yesterday and today and forever" (Hebrews 13:8).

Prayer: I stand in awe of Your wisdom Lord, from before the foundation of the world to the end of time. You are the answer to meeting all I long for. Thank You. In Jesus name, amen.

Unwise thoughts: Refusing to acknowledge God's truth

Preserve Sound Judgment

⌾⌾⌾

My Son preserve sound judgment and discernment, . . . they will be life for you.

—Proverbs 3:21–22

*B*izarre! This tragic and absurd performance rated high on the list of illogical, yet triggered a certain amount of humor. The police cruiser was chasing a vehicle, but instead of going faster it was slowing down—it ran out of gas! No problem though; the driver gets out and pushes his car as he steers it. The police approach the car as they watch this outlandish situation. When they move toward the suspect to apprehend him, the driver tells them to "back off." What! He must have thought this was a game to play. He found out differently when the police cuffed his hands and threw the culprit in the squad car.

Preposterous, you might conclude, but decisions like this by people who have no discernment are repeatedly made. This driver made a wrongful life decision. Not wanting to be caught for it, he conceived an aggressive plan to outrun the police. He certainly didn't have sound judgment and didn't even recognize his folly or the seriousness of his situation. By his actions and wrongful decision he quickly learned what the consequences of his outrageous, dim-witted choice would reap.

Preserving sound judgment involves really attempting to *know* and *understand* a situation so that we can make a correct decision. It helps us to separate the right way from the wrong way, so we can clearly assess any problem or needed direction before us and make a wise and beneficial choice for our lives—God's choice. Yes, "The wise in heart are called discerning" (Proverbs 16:21).

We gain this awareness as we intentionally seek and *walk in the Lord* for our everyday right choices. Solomon's insightful words are, we can "go our way in safety, and your foot will not stumble" and "when you lie down, your sleep will be sweet" (Proverbs 3:23). When you go to bed at night you won't have to question if you have made the right decision, or lie awake with your stomach churning.

When we have discernment and sound judgment from the Lord, it brings peace in the midst of the storms of life, including difficult relationships, job situations, rebellious children or financial needs. With *His peace* we will "Have no fear of sudden disaster or the ruin that overtakes the wicked" (Proverbs 3:25). We don't always have to be looking over our shoulder to see if someone is going to apprehend us for some wrong conclusions we've made.

We will find discernment and sound judgment awaiting us when we purposely set time aside for God's Word. He desires to lead and direct, but *you* must be *willing to spend time seeking Him*. Proverbs 3:26 sums it up with this: "for the Lord will be your confidence and will keep your foot from being snared." Sound judgment *can be yours today*.

Prayer: Lord, I have made some ridiculous decisions in my life that have brought me pain because I lacked discernment or sound judgment. I want You to be my director in the future decisions I make. In Jesus name, amen.

Unwise actions: Making decisions without seeking the Lord.

Taken for Granted

Do not withhold good from those who deserve it, when it is in your power to act.

—Proverbs 3:27
(Read also: 3:28)

Martha, a compassionate teacher, taught a Sunday school class of active junior-high girls. The necessity to implant the Word of God in these lives was crucial to her. She committed herself to train them challenging them with contests and activities—and, it worked. Martha influenced many of these young teen girls, including myself, to accept and serve Jesus Christ. I don't believe she was praised or appreciated for her time and efforts, but she *willing* consented. I have thought of Martha often and even though I would only keep in contact with her at Christmas, I have told her many times how much of an impact she was on my life.

We take a lot of people for granted. They are always there making life better for us, helping in their particular gifting—a teacher, pastor, co-worker, parent, even our children, spouse, or friend. Most of these people certainly never consider acting out of praise or desire for recognition. It is worthwhile for us to remember not to "withhold good from those who deserve it when it is in your power to act."

Acknowledgment is one reason why many businesses take special occasions to honor individuals when they have gone the extra mile. Some companies recognize a heroic act. Other individuals are faithful to do their best in what they always do, yet are never noticed. They too need acknowledgment—a surprise birthday party, a special treat, an invitation to breakfast, a card of thanks, or other special ways.

Showing appreciation requires a positive mind-set. Seeing the negative side of someone is always easy, but appreciating the positive tendencies brings better results. Do you appreciate the good things done by individuals in your family and compliment them on it? Have you ever considered the sacrifices, work and love your parents have placed into your life? Don't withhold thankfulness. A pastor can be a tremendous influence in your spiritual growth.

It wasn't until September 11, 2001, and the bombing of the World Trade Center that people fully appreciated the work of the firemen in our country. Those who give of themselves, demonstrate God's love, give beneficial advice, or show care and concern, need to know that they are valued. When we view people with the eyes of Jesus, our perspective changes away from our problems, and ourselves. This perception helps us to recognize the blessings we can also give away.

We all have something that doesn't require much for us to give— love and kindness. Use the Golden Rule—do unto others as you would have them do unto you. Everyone seems to respond in a more positive way when they are occasionally appreciated or acknowledged. No one likes to be taken for granted. Today think of someone whom you can acknowledge and do something special for them.

Prayer: Lord, help me today to see someone I should acknowledge to show Your love and kindness in the way You would want me to. In Jesus name, amen.

Unwise thoughts: Withholding your power to act.

Pick a Side

The Lord's curse is on the house of the wicked, but he blesses the home of the righteous.

—Proverbs 3:33
(Read also: 3:34–35, Proverbs 11:21))

A close examination of the descendents of a well-known *Christian* living *a few* centuries ago established that his offspring became leaders, lawyers, presidents of universities, and good citizens contributing their time and talents to society. Another name analyzed was taken of descendents of a *notorious killer* during the same time frame. This analysis found that his brood became thieves, robbers, killers, and instead of benefiting society, burdened it with the cost of their evil deeds and the expense of imprisonment.

A striking difference between things being compared—is a contrast. These differences such as good and evil, brainless and wise, are as *unlike* as cold and hot, a beautiful sunset and a raging storm. There is no possible way to connect these distinctions. Solomon contrasts the wicked and the righteous, the mocker and the humble, the wise and the fool. Which side are you on?

Wise	Unwise
Proverbs 3:33 The home of the righteous is blessed.	- The home of the wicked is cursed.

Proverbs 3:34 God gives grace to the humble.	- He mocks the mocker.
Proverbs 3:35 The wise inherit honor.	- Fools He holds up to shame.

The Psalmist pictures for us, "Blessed is the man (person) who fears the Lord . . . His children will be mighty in the land; the generation of the upright will be blessed" (Psalm 112: 1–2). The unwise individual, who mocks the things of God, also scorns and ridicules His goodness. Such people are deceived and spiritually blind "not realizing that God's kindness leads you (or them) toward repentance," the apostle Paul shares (Romans 2:4). God in turn "mocks proud mockers" and pours out His wrath on them. But He gives unearned but *abundant* favor to those whose heart is *humble* before Him.

The definition of honor is—high regard or respect. This is what the wise inherit when they serve the Lord, walk in His directions, and commit to keeping His commandments. God's commandments give us vital help and positive directions on how to live. When we earnestly rely on them, they will guide our steps and direct us in wisdom. Following God wholeheartedly, we will also receive honor—from our colleagues, our family, friends and coworkers who recognize our good judgment.

The unwise fool doesn't know the distinction of right from wrong and persists to make unwise choices. Therefore, "fools he holds up to shame." Their deeds become known and the consequences are a soiled reputation, sometimes destroyed families, and broken lives.

The contrast between these scriptures is very striking, so make your decision and pick a side—the wise or the unwise. The Psalmist cries out, "How can I repay the Lord for all his goodness to me? His answer—put God's Word into practice (Psalm 116:12,14). Be God-wise today.

Prayer: Lord, I too realize how good You have been to me. I pick Your wisdom and choose Your righteousness. Thank You for all that is available for me in You. In Jesus name, amen.

Unwise actions: Scorning God and His wisdom.

Listen and Heed

Listen, my sons to a father's instruction; pay attention and gain understanding.

—Proverbs 4:1 (Read also: 4:2–9)

$\mathcal{S}$olomon heeded King David's counsel when he entreated him to "attend and learn intelligence: I (David) give you good counsel, turn not from my teaching" (Proverbs 4:2). He encouraged Solomon to "Hold fast my words in *your mind*. Keep my commandments and live" (Proverbs 4:4, from An American translation). "Get wisdom," his father advised, "get understanding: *forget it not*" (Proverbs 4:5). He was saying to his son Solomon, *listen* and *pay attention* to what I have to say; it is good and wise counsel for you.

At the age of 17 Todd nearly died during his third drug overdose in two years, after ingesting a bag of hallucinogenic mushrooms and taking amphetamines. Todd never thought he would live past his teens. He was just minutes from death. Todd had been in and out of jail since he dropped out of school in the eighth grade when he was sentenced to 14 months in jail.

At his dilapidated house he was startled with a loud knock at the back door. He thought it was a drug bust; instead a huge bearded man named John with a white Bible under his arm bursts in. A former addict and friend of Todd's current drug dealer, John approaches him and begins to give him a dynamite sermon. Todd screams he doesn't want to hear any more. John proceeds to plop the Bible into Todd's lap and instructs him to close his eyes, open the Bible and put his finger on a word and read it.

Todd is curious and yet wants to get rid of him so he did what he was told. Opening the Bible, he put his finger on a word and froze as he read the words—"Listen now." The fear of God came over him as it spoke to something inside of him and he instantly had a spiritual birth—on the spot. Immediately he was delivered from drugs and alcohol without going through any withdrawal symptoms.

For the next three months after work, Todd spent 4 to 12 hours a day in Bible study and prayer. Because of his hunger for more of God he would cry out for the Holy Spirit to work in his life. It was almost like he was getting Bible school training as he pressed in to encounter more from God, for hours each day. If we hunger and thirst after righteousness, we will be filled, God's Word encourages. Todd found that to be true. A remarkable transformation began to take place in this 17-year-old former drug addict.

Today Todd, now approaching thirty-some, is an evangelist who travels around the world with signs and miracles following him as he shares the hope and promises of Jesus. "*Listen now*, pay attention and gain wisdom and understanding" are words more powerful than gold or diamonds. Take heed of them today as you grasp His Word.

Prayer: Father, I hunger for more of You, and to listen and heed Your Word. Please strengthen this desire in me today. In Jesus name, amen.

Unwise actions: Carelessly rejecting God's concern for you.

Guard Your Heart

Above all else, guard your heart, for it is the wellspring of life.

—Proverbs 4:23

*I*n our modern-day world the heart is understood as three separate areas of our human make-up: mind, emotions, and will. Biblically though, all three were intertwined in their usage. Out of the heart comes a range of emotions—joy, sorrow, fear, worry, distress, passion, anguish and so much more.

Through our technologies today opportunities abound for us to consume vast amounts of helpful or unhealthy influences. It is through the *eye gate of our heart* that we absorb these influences. Watching the news can cause us to be anxious; hearing the negative report of the stock market can bring indigestion; and reading the newspaper or world report magazines causes worry to run rampant about what the future will hold.

We may partake of things that make us feel filthy. The images we see on television will sometimes hit at our moral code of conduct. If we continue to allow the world's influence in our lives, our hearts will be burdened and that pressure will affect our whole being. Computers are wonderful in many ways, however they also have more information than necessary at times and some sites should not be accessed. Many have fooled around with pornography sites, and their hearts are now in tyranny to the enemy of their souls.

Guard and keep a watch on what you permit into your mind, emotions and will. Jesus called a crowd of people to Him and commanded, "Listen to me, everyone, and understand this. Nothing outside a man can make him 'unclean' by going into him. Rather, it is what comes out of a man that makes him 'unclean'" (Mark 7:14). Later when His disciples inquired the meaning of the parable He explains, "Don't you see that nothing that enters a man from the outside can make him 'unclean'? For it doesn't go into his heart but into his stomach, and then out of his body. For from within, *out of men's hearts*, come evil thoughts, sexual immorality, theft, murder, adultery, greed and malice, deceit, lewdness, envy, slander, arrogance and folly. All these evils come from inside and make a man 'unclean'" (Mark 7:18–23).

Reread the above listing over again. Is there something there that you have allowed to enter your heart to cause you to sin—greed, deceit, slander, envy or others? Apart from God, man is destined to doing corrupt things. But God's answer is a transformed heart, forgiven and cleansed on a *daily basis*. This daily commitment is crucial to a healthy spiritual life and is also essential to obedience. God will then create a desire in us to aggressively *walk in Him* and *serve* Him, against the backdrop of this world's values. It is He who will help you *guard your heart* for it is "the wellspring of life" to you.

Prayer: Lord, I realize I have accepted things in my heart that are not pleasing to You. I plead Your forgiveness. I want to rely on You to help guard my mind, emotions and will. Thank You. In Jesus name, amen.

Unwise actions: Dropping your guard.

What Did You Say?

Put away perversity from your mouth; keep corrupt talk far from your lips.

—Proverbs 4:24
(Read also: Proverbs 11:12)

*F*lipping through the television channels recently, I sat appalled at the violent, filthy profanity I heard on so many programs. Cringing at it, I wondered why? "This level of vulgar language had been restrained before. Why do they need to resort to it now" I thought. Then I vaguely remembered an article in the news. It told that the Federal Communications Commission, the agency watchdog for on-air language, decreed a new era in American public language usage because it found this language to be "contemporary community standards." That means, this is what our society is speaking and will accept now!

The tongue, yet so small, can speak both excellent and helpful words, and yet such vile ones. James, the brother of Jesus put it this way: "The tongue also is a fire, a world of evil among the parts of the body. It corrupts the whole person, sets the whole course of his life on fire, and is itself set on fire by hell" (James 3:6). *It corrupts the whole person.* Had you ever thought of it that way?

Notice that when filthy words are expressed, countless times the name of the Lord is misused. God's commandment says that He "will not hold anyone guiltless who misuses his name" (Deuteronomy 5:11). God entreats us to use His name with reverence.

The next generation is watching us. Innocent children who are viewing television, accept much of what they hear and will model the same. They watch you too and duplicate *your* walk and talk. Children are being inwardly corrupted by not being taught that the detrimental words they speak will "set the whole course of *their* life on fire." Are you adding to that? Or are you teaching them that the lewd, vulgar words of this world are not pleasing in God's sight? We are not only to teach them but also protect them from these ungodly influences as well. That could mean turning off the television if needed, and guarding our own lips.

Proverbs advises, "Good sense is on the lips of the intelligent, but folly lies in the talk of senseless men" (Proverbs 10:13 Moffat). The apostle Paul tells the Colossians to rid themselves of "filthy language" from their lips (Colossians 3:8).

We entered into a spiritual realm when we received Christ. His desires for our lips are clean, skillful, and encouraging words. Foul words pull down and degrade people. They corrupt the whole person. There is a saying—garbage in, garbage out. *Our words* are to be praises to Him, plus they should be confessing the name of Jesus to others. When we desire to please God, we will invite Him to clean up our speech. Then be wise, put away rotten words so it won't be said of you—"What did he say?"

Prayer: Father, I do not want to corrupt others or myself. The Psalmist prayed, "May the words of my mouth . . . be pleasing in your sight," I desire that as well. Thank You for Your help. In Jesus name, amen.

Unwise actions: Using corrupt language.

The Path

Let your eyes look straight ahead, fix your gaze directly before you. Make level paths . . . and take only ways that are firm. Do not swerve to the right or to the left.

—Proverbs 4:25–27

*U*pon our inquiry, the campground host informed us of an easy wooded hike that would take us up the mountain to a stunning lake. With a little hesitancy my husband and I, our three girls, and our dog drove to the trail, parked, and headed out to conquer it. The first section was a thick beautiful forest. We cautiously stepped over a picturesque gurgling river, and soon embarked on the rugged ascent to our destination. The next hour and a half we trudged up zigzag switchbacks, stumbled over exposed roots, balanced on rocks through another river, and landed above the treetops.

While resting in an open area, we encountered some individuals who had reached the top and inquired of them the distance to get to this awesome lake. When we heard that we were only half-way to this treasured view we did some serious thinking for about two minutes, then decided that our desire to see it wasn't that pressing—and turned around and scrambled down.

Stationed on our paths of life there are many rocks to negotiate, switchbacks, and exposed roots. These include harsh disappointments, upsetting discouragements, irritations and bleeding hurts that are attributed to marriage infidelity, financial losses, disobedient children, moral failures or sibling rivalry. The fallout of these can produce bitterness, hatred, rebellion, or lack of self-esteem. Some of these obstacles represent unwise or foolish choices you made that aimed you on the wrong path. They're like exposed roots that one stumbles over.

"Let your eyes look straight ahead" is good advice. Straight ahead means keeping our *focus on Jesus*, fixing our gaze on Him. A difficult job situation or a loss of employment can be very stressful. It seems like a switchback climb each day. When your focus is on Jesus you won't stumble over the rocks, those problems life deals to you. Search God's Word for guidance and open your heart to sense His will in *each* circumstance. He will keep *you*r foot steady and also partner with you as your souls companion on your rugged pathway. The prophet Isaiah reminds, "The path of the righteous is level: O upright One, *you make the way of the righteous smooth*" (Isaiah 26:7).

The forest path we tramped on, at times, had a steep drop off so that we carefully choose our footing. Vigilant footing in our spiritual life is also needed. "Do not swerve to the right or the left," verse 27 encourages us. Don't mentally enlarge your problems so that you become overwhelmed. That produces unstable footing and can excite you to take the illogical direction on your path (verse 27). Instead, earnestly linger for a while with God in prayer. He will keep your foot firm on the right path—His path.

Prayer: I fix my gaze on You today Lord, and wait on You in prayer. Keep me focused, on level footing each day so that I do not stumble. In Jesus name, amen.

Unwise actions: Taking my own path.

You're Being Watched

For a man's ways are in full view of the Lord.

—Proverbs 5:21
(Read also: Proverbs 16:2, 21:2)

*A*mazing satellites! How many of us, some years ago, would have guessed that the future would hold such an instrument propelled into orbit miles above us that could see objects very clear on earth? Now there is another, newer development called an air-drone, a man, manipulated smaller aircraft that can fly 20,000 feet above enemy territory with a meticulous camera that can scout out every small movement below.

One miraculous camera that has been in existence for thousands of years has an even better lens than any we may have developed today. This lens sees past all the visual objects and right into the very heart. Proverbs 15:3 warns us how completely visible that is: "The eyes of the Lord are *everywhere*, keeping watch on the wicked and the good."

The Lord's lenses observe your angry tantrums, the acute mistreatment of the children He has given you, any sexual misconduct, malicious words to your spouse, stealing, taking advantage of people to get your way, excessive time spent watching television, or the busyness of your life. Because we *seemingly* get away with these actions without any negative consequences, we convince ourselves that these dealings are justifiable. "Don't remind me that I'm being watched" is our attitude. We mortals like to have things hidden for no one to witness. But, *everything* is in "full view" of Him.

Yet the Lord sees even deeper: "The lamp of the Lord searches the spirit of man, it searches out his inmost being" (Proverbs 20:27). Even "our motives are weighed by the Lord" (Proverbs 16:2). These include your motives for *serving* Jesus, attending God's house, helping your neighbor, your work ethic on your job, loving your husband, ministering to the unsaved, giving offerings to the church or serving on a lay committee. The wise person will take a spiritual account, from time to time, to ask,—*"Are my motives right before God* in these diverse areas of my life?"

If the Lord observes and is familiar with everything about us, then He *"understands every motive* behind our thoughts" as well (1 Chronicles 28:9). He knows if we are artificial with Him or if we actually *are focused* on serving Him with our whole being. If all is in full view of Him, we certainly can't conceal anything deep in our hearts either.

The wise believer wants God's full approval in every part of their life. It's His *power* working in you that makes it possible to desire *His* right motives, which are important to Him. He will forgive anyone who will come to Him with a repentant heart. He *delights* to look on *you* with pleasure, seeing His child alive in Him, acting out His Word, and proving His work through you as a testimony to your world of influence.

Prayer: Lord, I know I can't hide anything from You. I now ask You to search my inmost being and check my motives, reveal them to me. I desire Your look of approval today. In Jesus name, amen.

Unwise actions: Continuing to have wrong motives.

Ensnared

My son, if you have put up security for your neighbor, if you
have struck hands in pledge for another . . . ensnared by words
of your mouth . . . then do this . . . to free yourself.

—Proverbs 6:1–2
(Read also: Proverbs 11:15)

*Y*ou can kiss that money goodbye," exclaimed Trent as Ken's cousin
Bill walked out of the house. Bill claimed he needed earnest money
on a down payment for an older house his family was hoping to buy.
"Could you help us out?" Bill pleaded. Ken knew about the need and
thought this would be an opportunity to help him. Good-hearted Ken
couldn't say no to his cousin's request, even though he had reservations
about the transaction. Then Bill backed out of the deal and lost the
earnest money as well. Bill forfeited the money to pay back Ken and
soon began avoiding him. The relations between cousins turned tensed
and eventually caused a division in their related families.

Solomon's wise counsel is this—Don't pledge or make a financial
agreement to give friends, acquaintances, or relatives expecting to
receive it paid back. Or don't sign any contract along with them that
would make you responsible for their debt in any way. That is, unless
you don't care if you are repaid. These erroneous decisions could lead
to a loss of lifetime friendships or a great disagreement in family relationships, hurts, arguments, and unforgiveness. Misjudged decisions
create snares and many unpleasant scenes. You may be aware of some

situations that were a positive experience, but that is not usually the case.

This doesn't mean, though, that we should refuse someone who is in real need of the basic necessities of life. Rather, we should give to those less fortunate, not expecting anything back. This thought is not addressed in the original concern.

Here is a caution: "A man *lacking* in judgment strikes hands in pledge and puts up security for his neighbor" (Proverbs 17:18). Those who lack judgment are incapable of judging a situation correctly. This causes them to make foolish decisions. Consequences of those decisions can bring them heartaches that originate from their good intent, but poor judgment.

You might inquire then, "How should I answer such a request?" It is wise to ask that question previous to its happening so that you may be equipped to answer discreetly. *Hasty decisions* cause undue stress, so simply respond that you would consider their request as you think and pray about it. God declares He will grant us wisdom when we ask of Him. Learning to rely on Jesus and seeking His wisdom will relieve us from making mistakes.

As you earnestly pray and diligently search His Word to speak to you, He will definitely present you with direction and words to speak. God will also prepare the heart of that individual so they are able to accept your answer when given in the *right* spirit. This wisdom will keep you from being ensnared in any questions in life.

Prayer:　　Thank You Father, that I can come to You and receive the wisdom I need for each decision I will encounter today. I accept it from You. In Jesus name, amen.

Unwise action: Going ahead without God's direction.

Ant or Sluggard

Go to the ant, you sluggard; consider its ways and be wise!
—Proverbs 6:6
(Read also: Proverbs 14:23)

It was one of those remarkable tranquil, warm spring days—except for the irritating flies. Dave entertained himself by killing a few flies, whisking them to the ground, and observed as the ants in the grass tried to drag and tug the dead fly, an object greater than themselves, away for food. Nothing hindered them—no stones in their way, no hills to climb, or no obstacle. They were persistent in their task, he noticed. Methodically they accomplished what sometimes seemed insurmountable for their size and kept at it until the task was finished.

Have you ever passed a work site along the road and noticed that only two out of four were working, while the others were just standing around and getting paid for it? Do you know that *accountability, dependability, commitment* and the *responsibility* we put into *any* work we do is important to God? Proverbs gives us the ant as an example.

Solomon described going past a vineyard. He noticed that thorns had grown up everywhere and that the ground was covered with weeds. He concluded it to be the vineyard of a sluggard, of one who is lazy and lacks judgment, because he wasn't wise enough to know that his neglect would bring him into poverty (Proverbs 24:30–34).

The apostle Paul instructs the Colossians, "Whatever you do, work at it with all your heart, as working for the Lord, not for men"

(Colossians 3:23). When the boss is around, many are careful to be seen diligently working, but if he is not present—party time may be the atmosphere.

A Christian young man worked for a meat sausage plant. One responsibility he had was working alone in a big freezer at the back of the building. From a distance the boss would occasionally observe him working. One time his boss commented, "I know I can rely on you to do the job even while you are away from your co-workers. You don't fool around, you get it done." His testimony of being dependable, accountable and persistent in finishing a task, led the boss to hire other Christians.

The apostle Paul reminds the Colossians, "It is the Lord Christ you are serving" (Colossians 3:24). "You mean that in *all* my work I am serving the Lord?" you may ask. Exactly. *All* is included in "*Whatever* you do"—and we are told to do it with joy. Think about it. What way brings a greater testimony—the "ant" work ethic or the lazy "sluggard" work ethic? Which one are you?

Christ's work ethic for us is different from the world's work ethic because we don't work for men—we serve Him. It brings respect from outsiders and an opportunity to be a visual testimony of Christ working in you. Consider the ant's ways and *be wise*.

Prayer: To be wise in heart is my desire, O Lord. I ask for help in my visual testimony that I may show others You are the one I serve. In Jesus name, amen.

Unwise actions: Sluggards destroy their testimony.

Arrogance

> There are six things the Lord hates, seven that are detestable to him: haughty eyes, . . . a man who stirs up dissension among brothers.
>
> —Proverbs 6:16–19

Sin never travels alone. It always takes a partner in its wickedness" is a noted saying. Sin's partners in these verses are haughty eyes and one stirring up strife. "Haughty eyes" for us today can be interpreted in this definition: showing great pride in oneself and *contempt for others*; *arrogance*.

Here are a few ways arrogance and contempt flaunt themselves. You might be able to add some along with these:

Extreme pride of one's tremendous abilities
Superiority because of stockpiled riches
Arrogant rebellion demonstrated by arguments, fights, etc.
The "I can do without you" attitude, conceit
Snobbery toward those less fortunate
Extremely judgmental, or very controlling attitude
Arrogance is demonstrated by anyone who instills strife within any
     group, family, adult siblings, or church family

Haughtiness and stirring up strife are detestable to the Lord. He hates them, as Solomon states in Proverbs 8:13 "I (wisdom) hate pride and arrogance, evil behavior and perverse speech." Why? Strife and arrogance are not from the Lord. These two partners stir contentions, ill feelings, quarrels, arguments or splits in families, siblings or churches. They do not bring peace. Satan our enemy knows that only too well and will keep these obnoxious attitudes brewing in those willing to be used by him.

Allowing strife in your relationship(s) causes you to lose your focus on the spiritual work God has for His people, and it hinders the work God commends for your life as well. God desires His peace to be among His people. He encouraged the disciples with these words: "Peace I leave with you; my peace I give you" (John 14:27). Peace is kept when our mind and heart are steadfast on Him, as Isaiah the prophet counsels us, "You will keep in perfect peace him whose mind is steadfast, because he (she) trusts in you" (Isaiah 26:3–4).

Because the arrogant, and unwise self-centered person(s) needs an attitude and heart adjustment, we are to pray that God will do just that in His perfect way. Don't lend to this arrogance by agreeing or accepting his or her attitude or making excuses for it. The wise will also talk less and pray more, which will help them display the fruit of peace.

The apostle Paul encourages the Colossians to, "Bear with each other and forgive whatever grievances you may have against one another. *Forgive as the Lord forgave you*" (Colossians 3:13–14). He adds to *"put on love,"* demonstrating it to be the adhesive glue for perfect unity among your church family, siblings, spouse or other individuals. Receive that love in the presence of Jesus.

God hates arrogance and strife, but He loves you and me. He wants His peace to fill your heart and mind right now. Claim that peace in Jesus' name for every situation where arrogance and strife live.

Prayer:　　Yes Lord, you know my frustration with _____. (fill in) I claim peace instead of the arrogance and strife that has kept me in turmoil for so long. Instill in me Your peace as well. In Jesus name, amen.

Unwise actions: Continued strife brings God's judgment.

Wicked Scheming

There are six things the Lord hates, . . . hands that shed innocent blood, a heart that devises wicked schemes, feet that are
quick to rush into evil, . . .

—Proverbs 6:17–18

$\mathcal{F}$orty minutes outside the capital city of Freetown, Sierra Leone,
West Africa, people live in thatched-roof huts, farm small plots with
simple tools and live in primitive conditions. In 1984 Joe came with
15 other members of his church and built an orphanage, literally
forming bricks from mud to build this project. He found the work so
enriching for him, he traveled back about twice a year bringing sup-
plies and constructing other needed structures. Joe considered these
people his second family.

Seven years later civil war pounded this country. Machete-wielding
rebels, looting, burning and destroying everything and everyone, ac-
costed many defenseless villages. They chopped off limbs of thousands
of men, women and children. After the war Joe went back to this second
family, rebuilt the orphanage, and constructed the urgent project of a
hospital to fit prosthetics for the amputees.

Our news media and technologies bring us many heart-wrenching
atrocities. They inform us of individuals who devise (concoct) wicked
schemes contrary to God's Word, then swiftly execute their methods
through murders, rape, stealing, or kidnapping. The three schemes

listed in our scripture cohabit in evilness compelling shocking consequences.

Some of you were involved in such damaging actions in your former carnality—*but now* you are cleansed in heart by the blood of Christ, forgiven from the past and filled with a new direction in life. These acts of wickedness are not to be known of believers. The apostle Paul admonishes the Ephesians, "I tell you this, . . . that you must no longer live as the Gentiles (unsaved) do. They are darkened in their understanding and *separated from the life of God* because of the ignorance that is in them due to the *hardening of their hearts*" (Ephesians 4:17,18).

In writing his epistle James declares, "each one is tempted when, by his own evil desire, he is dragged away and enticed. Then after *desire* has conceived, it gives birth to sin" (James 1:14–15).

Salvation brings forgiveness, but our active daily discipline in God's Word and valued time in His presence keep us from yielding our thoughts to sin's temptations and evil schemes. Heed this wise believers, "live by the Spirit (of God) and you will not gratify the desires of the sinful nature. For the sinful nature desires what is contrary to the Spirit and the Spirit what is contrary to the sinful nature. They are in *conflict to each other*" (Galatians 5:16–17).

You choose to daily renew your mind in His Word; you choose to *reject* the scheming sinful desires and to radiate God's principles. If any of these thoughts arise, rebuke them in the name of Jesus. Then purposely hit the delete button of your mind. Don't let the enemy of your soul trip you. Your wise decision will please Him as you determine to walk in His strength.

Prayer: In Jesus name I choose to refuse sinful thoughts and I long to live by the Spirit. Strengthen me Father, in this resolve. Thank You, amen.

Unwise thoughts: Concocting wicked schemes.

Affairs

For these commands are a lamp . . . keeping you from the immoral woman (man), from the smooth tongue of the wayward wife (husband). Do not lust after her (his) beauty.
—Proverbs 6:23,24
(Read also: Proverbs 7:4–26)

According to a poll, 35 percent of the people who use personal ads for dating are already married. The percentage of married people having affairs has increased dramatically. You may have a good marriage or one that is unsatisfactory to you. Affairs are rampant today.

Affairs don't just "happen" though. They are conceived in the heart and mind when one continues to think and dwell on them (James 1:15). The longing grows, like a baby in a mother's womb, as you cuddle those thoughts until it brings you to actual behavior. People are then willing to pay any price to have their desire fulfilled and hope they can get away with it.

"Can a man (woman) scoop fire into his (her) lap without his (her) clothes being burned?" Proverbs asks (6:27). Playing around with sin is like playing with fire. *Any* sexual encounter outside of marriage is detestable to God. According to His Word, the person "who commits adultery lacks judgment: whoever does so destroys himself (herself)" (Proverbs 6:32).

The apostle Paul counsels Christians, "But among you there should not be even a hint of sexual immorality . . . because these are improper for God's holy people" (Ephesians 5:3). God knew the devastation it would bring—broken trust, shame, your dignity destroyed, possible loss of your job, and for a spouse, broken vows and a devastated and hurting family.

Again the apostle Paul warns, "It is God's will that you should . . . avoid sexual immorality, that each of you should learn to control his (her) own body in a way that is holy and honorable, not in passionate lust like the heathen, who do not know God. For God did not call us to be impure but to live a holy life" (1 Thessalonians 4:3–4,7).

How do you keep from falling into this pit of sin? Scripture gives us some tips. (1) Colossians 3:5 instructs that *you* are to *put to death* "whatever belongs to your earthly nature: sexual immorality, impurity, lust, evil desires . . ." *You stop* any lustful desires right at the onset by having scripture ready to think on whenever you are tempted. (2) If you are married, work to *reconnect that love relationship* you first had with your spouse, by *spending time with each other.* (3) If you need help contact trained Christian counselors.

Wise people "fear the Lord" and seek *His power* to overcome any unhealthy sexual desires. *Forgiveness* and *empowerment* can be yours as you "live by the Spirit" so that "you will not fulfill the desire of the sinful nature" (Galatians 5:16). Your answer is not another affair. It is seeking Jesus with all your heart. Today stop any lustful desires not pleasing to God.

Prayer: Jesus, I have been wrong in my thoughts and actions. I desire my body to be holy and honorable in Your sight. Empower me to put to death the desires of my sinful nature. In Jesus name, amen.

Unwise action: To continue my immoral ways or actions.

Long for and Seek it

Does not wisdom call out? Does not understanding raise her voice? To you, O men, I call out. You who are simple, gain prudence; you who are foolish, gain understanding.

—Proverbs 8:1,4,5
(Read also: Proverbs 8:6–21)

There's a parade coming. Let's go out to see it. Here, sit on the curb with me. Look, someone's carrying a hefty oversized banner. Written on it are gigantic words, "WISDOM" and "UNDERSTAND-ING." Notice that behind the banner is a BIG four-sided wagon with contrasting words on each side. First, Truth or Falsehood. Then Justice or Wickedness. And see this one: Discerning or Foolishness. And Wow, big powerful words on this side—CHOOSE INSTRUCTION, CHOOSE KNOWLEDGE. The words shout at us. They are almost blinding they're so brilliant. The wagon has silver and gold medallions that dangle down on a pole along each side but they are so dull compared to the brilliance of the words of wisdom.

Here come two stately cadets holding a gold cloth inscribed with the words, "To fear the Lord is to hate evil" (Proverbs 8:13). That's right! Hate evil! And see what this next banner reads—Reject: Arrogance, Evil Behavior, Perverse Speech and Pride. I don't want these in my life. The giant posters in this parade have been helpful. They remind us to guard ourselves from these carnal thoughts. A discerning heart will lead you to sound judgment, and a craving for

God's guidance in your life. Wisdom is s-o-o valuable that it "is more precious than rubies, and nothing you (we) desire can compare with her" (Proverbs 8:11).

The parade is almost finished. A light approaching is really bright, fluorescent, glorious, and breathtaking, and I hear words spoken that shoot through me like an arrow. "Counsel and sound judgment are mine: *I have* understanding and power. Choose my instruction instead of silver, knowledge rather than choice gold" (Proverbs 8:14,10).

My heart is seized as I sense wisdom and I want to shout, "Yes, I want Your counsel and sound judgment. I long for spiritual understanding to guide my steps. I seek to find You, O Lord." I weep as I sense His presence and know that I want to seek more wisdom, understanding and knowledge. The parade is gone, but its presence lingers. I linger.

Is *your* desire to seek the riches of these life sustaining attributes? If so, you *can* gain them for the Word's wisdom encourages, "I love those who love me, and those *who seek me find me*. With me are riches and honor, enduring wealth and prosperity" (Proverbs 8:17–18).

In every decision made by you, both small and great, words you articulate, or answers you seek, you can petition for wisdom, understanding, and knowledge from God and He will freely give it. Your part is to *accept* and *act on* what you receive. Wisdom is before you. Acknowledge it as you seek the Lord.

Prayer: Lord, I am desperate for Your wisdom in my life. I long for spiritual understanding to guide me. I seek Your answer and will act on it. In Jesus name, amen.

Unwise actions: Hanging on to your unwise decisions.

𝒜-t-t-i-t-u-d-e

Whoever corrects a mocker invites insult; whoever rebukes a wicked man incurs abuse.

—Proverbs 9:7

𝓗is name was Buck. Several believers were handing out gospel tracts to people on a corner near a shopping area. Many received them and looked them over. I approached Buck to hand him the pamphlet and talk to him about Jesus. He became irate and lambasted me with all kinds of negative words regarding what he thought about my tract. He hurled it down stamping on it and spewing out all kinds of explicit foul language.

When he headed toward me, I backed away. My thoughts went back to something I had read—in ten minutes, a hurricane releases more energy than the entire world's nuclear weapons combined! That saying fit Buck that day. Proverbs 14:16 shares, "a fool is hot headed and reckless."

It is accurately acknowledged, "A fool finds no pleasure in understanding but delights in airing his own opinions" (Proverbs 18:2). "The way of the fool seems right to him" is his perception (Proverbs 12:15). Be aware though—don't argue with a fool, people standing by can't tell which is which. That must have been taken from Solomon's words, "Do not answer a fool according to his folly, or you will be like him yourself" (Proverbs 26:4). Mockers and fools, condemn themselves.

With a know-it-all attitude, Buck mocked at making amends for his sin. He rejected acknowledging Jesus Christ. The apostle Paul helps us to understand this as he taught the Corinthians, "The man (woman) without the Spirit does not accept the things that come from the Spirit of God, for they are foolishness to him (her), and he cannot understand them, because they are spiritually discerned" (1 Corinthians 2:14). Buck couldn't distinguish the Spirit.

Mankind is incapable of understanding spiritual values if the Spirit of God does not illuminate them. You may notice it by the way your neighbors or co-workers respond when they hear anything about God or the Bible. They have the world's understanding, which is so opposed to the spiritual, just as opposite as dark and light. The Psalmist reminds us, "Blessed is the man (woman) who does not walk in the counsel of the wicked . . . or sit in the seat of the mocker" (Psalm 1:1).

To reach people for Christ the soil of their heart needs to be prepared. The *most powerful way* to help prepare that soil is to (1) *pray for them* and (2) *live our lives according to God's Word in front of them.* For some mockers to receive the Word, heart preparation takes a long time. For others who are searching for real answers to life, preparation could be short. Don't waste your words on one who is belligerent, and has a rebellious attitude. You will only invite insult from them. But do speak to those whom God has placed in your path, after you have prayed and sensed their heart's soil is ready.

Prayer: Lord, I know a mocker _____ (put name) whom I pray for today. I ask that Your Spirit would prepare his/her heart so I can speak to them about You. In Jesus name, amen.

Unwise actions: Incurring the wrath of a mocker.

Wise Father, Wise Son

A wise son brings joy to his father, but a foolish son brings grief
to his mother. He who has a wise son delights in him.
                                                —Proverbs 10:1, 23:24
                                      (Read also: Proverbs 23:15–16)

*I*t was a gratifying picture of Dean in his cap and gown surrounded
by his proud parents, Rich and Jewel. The joy on each face was radi-
ant and beaming with delight on this happy occasion of graduation.
They had all worked hard for this moment, and looked forward to this
final accomplishment with much anticipation. It had eclipsed all their
expectations.

Rich and Jewel had some tricky challenges in Dean's earlier
years. He was a high-strung and determined kid demanding his
way many times. It was like guiding a galloping horse, maneuvering
around curves and corners to avoid many catastrophes. In his teens,
Dean got sidetracked with unwise friends, and the plan of graduation
was almost cancelled.

Spiritually wise parents (or caregivers) are needed to raise a wise
son or daughter in God's ways. He desires children to learn true godli-
ness and commitment to Him primarily from their parents' daily role
modeling. That means wise parents don't only talk about spiritual things
but *live out* God's Word. A godly father's input is of tremendous value
to a child in all stages of life.

To be a wise example involves gaining wisdom on a daily basis from God's Word and to be open to His leading. We make mistakes when we lean on our own understanding and *not His*. That doesn't mean we will be perfect and raise perfect children. Most of us start out without a clue as to how to raise a family. When we think *we* know best is when we have a tendency to make incorrect judgments. Good or bad, we raise our children the way we were raised. You are blessed if you had a godly example.

Today there are so many good helps for parents—books, articles, talk shows, seminars and retreats. If your child should heed the wrong advice from their peers, your call on heaven will be heard. He will give wisdom and understanding beyond your abilities. If they heed wisdom, they too will become wise and, like Dean, will obtain their targeted goal.

Those happy occasions when we see our children excel come with a price. We learn what it means to stick to the task even through difficult days. Persistence gains us much experience, and some gray hairs. We learn that raising children involves a lot of wisdom, understanding and sacrifice, plus running kids to activities. Two main bonuses come in raising a wise child: 1. Parents grow wise and gain spiritually as they lean on the Lord. 2. There's *joy* when you see your child become a wise and responsible adult because of your helpful input. Yes, it's worth it all! A God wise dad (and mom) is needed to raise a wise son.

Prayer: Thank You Father for wisdom to impart to my children so they gain spiritually and become responsible adults. Help my child to respond to Your wisdom implanted in my life today. In Jesus name, amen.

Unwise actions: Unwise fathers raise unwise children.

Memory of the Righteous

The memory of the righteous will be a blessing, but the name of the wicked will rot.

—Proverbs 10:7
(Read also: Proverbs 10:20–21,28)

Billions of people know the name of Billy Graham. His crusades and invitations for salvation have touched numerous lives. Mr. Graham's example of sharing Jesus has been noticed, admired and accepted by many in all walks of life from the president to the average person. It is true, "The mouth of the righteous brings forth wisdom" (Proverbs 10:31). We remember his righteous example as a blessing to us.

Thousands did not know Ross Simmons, my father-in-law, but he was known by acquaintances for his righteous example to his family. Others, to whom he *was* known as Pastor, were blessed by him as well. He willingly became a servant of God, serving his family first, then people's needs, praying for them and inviting them to know Christ more intimately in their lives. He taught his family to "fear the Lord" and seek Him.

Dad Simmons's example of serving his wife as she became an invalid, was a tremendous testimony to all around him. The residents in the nursing home came to know him as Pastor as well, and when he himself was elderly and moved into the nursing home he would stop and pray for individuals, sometimes right in the hall, and he experienced his greatest harvest there for the Lord. Proverbs 11:18 asserts, "He who sows righteousness reaps a sure reward."

It is excellent to recall the righteous, "but the name of the wicked will rot" (Proverbs 10:7). God hates wickedness. Even after many years, the mention of the name of Hitler brings a range of emotions to a countless number of people. Hitler's cruelty, killings, imprisonment of Jews and others, and his insane commands, brought ruin and separation into numerous families and countries. Memories of suffering, anguish and death will always trouble many of these people and their loved ones.

In the Old Testament one of the kings of Israel was named Manasseh. He reigned in Jerusalem for fifty-five years as one of Israel's most wicked kings. He bowed down and worshipped the gods of the wicked nations around him and sacrificed his sons on altars he built right in God's temple courts. The Bible recounts, "He did much evil in the eyes of the Lord, provoking him to anger" (2 Chronicles 33:6). His recorded memory will be: "Manasseh led Judah and the people of Jerusalem astray, so that they did more evil than the nations the Lord had destroyed before the Israelites" (2 Chronicles 33:9). Not a positive way to be remembered!

The memory of a righteous person is to be desired because, "The *hope* of the righteous ends in *gladness*" (Proverbs 10:28 RSV). Heaven is the hope of all the righteous. We are blessed when we have upright lives to emulate and look up to. Will the memory of your name bless others?

Prayer: Lord, my desire is to be remembered as one who has a relationship with You that will bless others. May my daily example be a blessing to many in my own world. In Jesus name, amen.

Unwise actions: Leaving a wicked legacy.

Take Advice

The wise in heart accepts commands, but a chattering fool comes to ruin.

—Proverbs 10:8
(Read also: Proverbs 13:13)

Neil fought in the Vietnam War. When he got out of service he became a biker, a tough and burly sort of guy, thrown in jail for brawls and drunkenness. When he sobered up they would let him go. Neil thought he knew it all and wouldn't listen to any advice. Neil eventually got married. An encounter he had in a traumatic accident deeply shook Neil, and through this dire situation he came to accept Christ.

Later in life Neil was diagnosed with diabetes. Ignoring helpful advice from his doctor, friends and family, Neil knew how to handle this, he thought, and disregarded their meaningful counsel. As he popped a sugar-coated candy in his mouth, he made the remark that he would let the disease just kill him quick. But that's not the way this disease works, it slowly rots away bodily members. Now as Neil is older, and somewhat wiser, there's a possibility of having a leg amputated because of this disease.

This opinion is given in Proverbs, "The way of the fool seems right to him (her), but a wise man (woman) listens to advice" (12:15). We chafe at wanting to accept good advice at times. "Don't tell me what I can or cannot do" is our attitude. "He who scorns instruction will pay for it" is the answer to this kind of thinking (Proverbs 13:13). There are people that have gone before us that have learned many lessons the hard way. They too thought they had all the answers to life and weren't willing to listen to any good counsel. That is, until they realized—they had been woefully wrong and very unwise. Now—they are *much* wiser.

Various times in our lives, the Lord aligns us with individuals who may help or give us just the right good advice for our questioning. A new mother may not have any clue of how to take care of her new baby, and an experienced grandma may live right next door. Or a dad doesn't know anything about being a father because he was raised in a home without a father. God might send a willing good role model into his life. Others may have gone through some of the same difficult health problems you might be facing and they may have very helpful suggestions for your situation.

Instead of having a know-it-all attitude, humble yourself before God, asking Him to send the best advice your way to help you. The Lord will assist you to recognize it. Open your eyes—it might be here already. Opportunities may also arise to share Jesus with whomever assists your need as well. Proverbs 19:20 recommends, don't be a chattering fool but, "Listen to advice and accept instruction, and in the end you will be wise."

Prayer:　　Yes, Lord, I humble myself before You and receive the help and advice for my situation through whatever individual(s) You choose. I thank You for it. In Jesus name, amen.

Unwise actions: Continue in your know-it-all attitude.

H-a-t-r-e-d

Hatred stirs up dissension, but love covers over all wrongs.

—Proverbs 10:12
(Read also: Proverbs 10:19)

Randy was hired as one of the coaches for a high school football team. He was given a three-year contract. Football regulations were important to Randy. In the coaches' chat meetings he realized some important regulations were being ignored. Randy questioned the reason for this and was given a brush-off type of answer. When this practice continued, he could not agree with this deception and wondered how he should handle it.

After he had been coaching for seven months he was released. At the time, he had no way to contest this decision. Because of their spiteful actions, other schools did not want to hire Randy, so he took other employment to support his wife and children. Randy was definitely hurting. He resented being dismissed for malicious reasons and as a Christian, he tried to resist the hate that was building up in his heart against his former employers. Randy had been wronged! His whole family was feeling the pressure of this difficult time.

Hatred keeps us from evaluating our situation in the correct way. It causes us to react in brainless frenzy. When dwelling on hatred, the heart and mind are hindered, blocking us to evaluate any situation wisely. An invisible net is wrapped around the longer hate is cuddled. As hatred is allowed to control you, the tighter the net gets and it always agrees to hate more. Everyone near feels the seething wrath of hatred. "Hatred stirs up dissension," the Scripture reminds us. It's hard to live with hate all the time. If allowed, it can destroy you and your loved ones.

Once hatred takes its hold, it doesn't easily let go. Only God's power can release and free you of all wounding offenses. Peace and healing *are* available. Your willingness to submit your hurts to God is your decision—or you can continue to pamper that hate and continue your downward spiral. When you submit it to the Lord, you must consciously supervise your thoughts on a daily basis. He will do His part and He will free that net of hatred around you. God does bring justice—but not always in our timing.

Eighteen months later, certain sports officials contacted Randy. They were investigating the misuse of regulations by his former coaches. Lawsuits and publicity brought everything out in the open. The coaches could no longer hide and be deceptive in their conniving former ways. Action was taken against them and all those involved. After the trial and justice was served, Randy received the severance pay due him and even more! Randy learned tremendous lessons as he saw God work on his behalf.

God's Word reminds us that what we sow, we reap. If we *sow hatred*, we reap the same. If we *sow love* and *forgiveness*, that's what we get. Love draws people to you and to Jesus.

Prayer: Father, break the net of hatred that entwines me. I no longer want to be under this bondage. Restore me in Your love so I can share it with others. In Jesus name, amen.

Unwise thoughts: Holding on to hatred.

Have You Heard . . . ?

Whoever spreads slander is a fool. When words are many, sin
is not absent, but he who holds his tongue is wise.
—Proverbs 10:18–19
(Read also: Proverbs 10:31–32)

$\mathcal{I}$t's game time shouted the hostess. She had ten people sit in a
circle. The object of the game was to start a saying and hurriedly pass
it to the person next to you until it was passed around the circle. The
saying was to be, "The pretty little girl had a big red umbrella." The
message started to be passed along with a lot of giggles and laughter.
By the end of the circle the saying translated into "The surly chilly girl
had a big rat relic." That example sealed what I had previously thought,
to guard my words and thoughtfully question what I hear.

Gossip. What's wrong with talking about someone behind his or
her back? I'm reminded of a friend that went into the hospital for an
appendix operation and later heard from others, that they were informed she had a leg amputated. Incredible you might say. Solomon
declares, "The words of a gossip are like choice morsels; they go down
to a man's (woman's) inmost parts" (Proverbs 18:8). Gossiping can be
very destructive. It may start out very innocent, but consider, "When
words are many, sin is not absent," as our scripture emphasizes.

Woe to those who are different or who have someone jealous
of them, like a co-worker, relative or companion. They can be torn
apart by cruel words, piece by piece, and thrown to the crocodile, as

a saying relates, and that person's reputation and life can be harmed or destroyed. Proverbs 3:29 warns, "Do not plot harm against your neighbor"—or anyone else for that matter.

James, in his epistle, writes, "Brothers (sisters), do not slander one another" (James 4:11). Again James pens, "With the same tongue we praise our Lord and Father, and with it we curse men. Out of the same mouth come praise and cursing . . . this should not be" (James 3:9–10). Our thoughtless tongue can separate close friends, betray a confidence, destroy someone's credibility, or cause quarrels. It also *breaks our fellowship with the Lord.*

If wood isn't added to a fire, it goes out. Likewise without gossip—lies, slander and quarrels will die down. Consider this, "He who guards his (her) mouth and his (her) tongue keeps himself (herself) from calamity," is wisdom we need to follow and put into practice (Proverbs 21:23). The Psalmist knew that what we say does not go unheard. "Before a word is on my tongue you know it completely, O Lord" (Psalm 139:4). The wisdom then is: *we are to resolve* that our mouth will not sin against God and our tongue will be kept from evil words.

The next time you hear someone say, "Have you heard . . ." remind yourself that, "he who holds his tongue is wise."

Prayer: Lord I have been reminded of the times I have spoken slander against one of Your creations. Forgive me. I resolve to speak wise and helpful words. Help me to keep a watch on my lips. In Jesus name, amen.

Unwise words: Slanderous words.

Willing to Be Instructed

❧

Instruct a wise man and he will be wiser still, teach a righteous man and he will add to his learning.

—Proverbs 9:9

*E*ducation begins at an early age—"Toes, eye, mouth;" "1, 2, 3;" "A, B, C;" "No, don't touch; the stove's hot." One little four-year-old girl told her Mommy, "I know a lot now, but when I go to school I'll know *everything*."

Since we never "know everything" it's necessary to continue to gain the necessary knowledge to sustain us in our world. Ross [10], Rachael [14], Sarah [16], and other classmates, proudly display the Principal's Award their school gives them for being on the Honor Roll. Receiving this award means they willingly have to agree to be instructed. These young people found being on the Honor Roll included hard work and self-discipline. Their parents' helpful input toward their education, gave them a *great* advantage.

An unwilling or rebellious student brings his or her own ruin. The following scripture sounds like experienced wisdom: "He who scorns instruction will pay for it," but "Whoever gives heed to instruction prospers" (Proverbs 13:13, 16:20). The appropriate knowledge we acquire can guide us in the right use of our godly gifts and talents. If a person can't be instructed from teachers who are interested in them, how then can they be instructed in God's laws?

Uzziah, at the age of 16, became king after his father was killed, and he reigned in Jerusalem for 52 years. The chronicles of his life began with "He did what was right in the eyes of the Lord. He sought God during the days of Zechariah, who instructed him in the fear of God" (2 Chronicles 26:1–5). Zechariah, a priest in the temple of God, taught young Uzziah the fear of the Lord, the crucial lessons necessary to succeed both in his kingdom and in his own life. And, "As long as he sought the Lord, God gave him success" (2 Chronicles 26:5). Uzziah's *willingness* was benefited by wise instruction that assisted him to obtain multiplied successes in his country's wars against his enemies, and also led to his kingdom becoming incredibly powerful.

King David, in writing his Psalms, reflects on instructions greater than any human teacher shares, "I have more insight than all my teachers, for I *meditate* on your *statutes*" (Psalm 119:99). The Psalmist goes on to share what he gains from these statutes: "Your commands make me wiser than my enemies, for they are ever with me. I gain understanding from your precepts" (Psalm 119: 98, 104).

Willing to be instructed, at *any* age, is necessary in *everyone's* life activities. We've all heard the saying—"It's never too old to learn." A *willing* individual can gain knowledge that will substantially profit them mentally and spiritually. Better yet, the wisdom and knowledge they receive from God's Word yields greater benefits—wise counsel to live godly lives.

Prayer: Thank You, Father, for all the instruction I received that has contributed to growth in my life. More important, I desire to meditate on Your Word, which teaches me Your wisdom and knowledge. In Jesus name, amen.

Unwise actions: Being unwilling to be instructed.

Humility Allows Wisdom

❧

When pride comes, then comes disgrace, but with humility comes wisdom.

—Proverbs 11:2
(Read also: Proverbs 8:12)

*I*t is impossible for the human mind to grasp the dreadful terror, enumerated deaths, and despicable atrocities that accompany dictator regimes. Saddam Hussein's system of power, control, imprisonment, and killings was very important to gain what he wanted. Other behaviors of controlling power surfaced, like pride, dishonesty, defiant arrogance, greediness, and evil revelations. He squeezed his people with military command and devastated their lives with his appalling demands. This dominant leader came to know a discreditable downfall.

The defeat that pride and arrogance reveals has been known from ancient times. Solomon recognized it and warns, "Before his downfall a man's (person's) heart is proud . . . a man's pride brings him low" (Proverbs 18:12, 29:23).

You might think, "Shouldn't everyone have some amount of pride?" That's right. The apostle Paul conveyed his feelings to the Corinthians, "I have confidence in you. I take great pride in you" (2 Corinthians 7:4). We all need to have a certain amount of pride, beneficial self-esteem, and a feeling that we have made positive accomplishments in our lives. The kind of pride discussed here is more than having a good personal feeling about everyday accomplishments. *It centers on a sin condition of the heart.*

Included in this sin condition of the heart is: *cultural pride*—which is strong, proud, and sometimes belligerent. This cultural, or nationality pride says, "I've been around for thousands of years." There is *denominational pride* that conveys superiority—we are the best and the only ones that have the true scope on spiritual things. There is *family pride*—keeping secrets of disgrace hidden yet eliciting prideful haughtiness. *Personal pride* reveals the hidden arrogance of the heart when proven through our actions and communications. But God declares, "I hate pride and arrogance, evil behavior and "perverse speech" (Proverbs 8:13).

Commit this to memory, "The Lord detests all the proud of heart" (Proverbs 16:5). His Word also reveals, "This is the one I esteem: he who is *humble and contrite in spirit*, and trembles at my word" (Isaiah 66:2). We can't *impress the Lord* by our foolish and erroneous intent and fantastic capabilities that bring us recognition in this world. *He is* stirred and interested in all who humble themselves, for those who rely on receiving continual sustenance and guidance from Him.

All individuals with their proud cultural attitudes, those with religious pride, the rebellious, the proud, boastful, and unrepentant will someday be required by God to *humbly* bow before Him, either here on earth or before Him in heaven. The Scripture suggests taking this action: arrogant, unrepentant pride brings disgrace, but "with humility comes wisdom." Humbly allow wisdom in you by recognizing His voice speaking to you to turn any proud, egotistical arrogance over to Him.

Prayer: Father, I lay any arrogant pride of _____ (name it) at Your feet and *humbly* submit to You. Your Word encourages me that You resist the proud but give favor to those who recognize You as Lord of their lives. Thank You, in Jesus name, amen.

Unwise actions: To continue in proud arrogance.

I-n-t-e-g-r-i-t-y

The integrity of the upright guides them.

—Proverbs 11:3
(Read also: I Chronicles 29:17)

*T*he young man was physically well built and very handsome. He had been sold by his jealous brothers, to a band of traveling traders and taken to Egypt. Potiphar, an Egyptian, purchased Joseph, son of Jacob, as a slave. When he saw that the Lord gave Joseph success in everything he did, Potiphar put him in charge of his entire household and entrusted to him everything he owned. Because of Joseph's integrity and the blessing of the Lord, that blessing also was transferred on Potiphar's house and everything he had (Genesis 39:1–6).

Integrity is a potent impact to your world of influence and a great testimony of your Christian life. In a recent Gallup poll of 1,509 Americans, 72 percent of us say our lives have meaning and purpose because of faith. But as believers *try to link their faith to everyday life*, many admit there is a gap between what they believe and how it is carried out.

What *is* a person of integrity? Here are just *a few* areas included in this word:

- One who can be trusted—who keep their word; what they say and do are the same
- who do more than is asked of them—who are consistent in paying their bills

- who are dependable and honest in everything—who do not consent to evilness
- who treat family and others with respect
- who demonstrates the love of Jesus with all they encounter.

Why then is it so hard to tie these actions with our faith in everyday life? We have some enemies of our soul that work against us. One enemy is the old sin nature that wants to still have preeminence in us. Another enemy is Satan—he hates when we spiritually succeed for Christ in *any way* and will stealthily attack us, discourage us, make us feel uncomfortable sharing the gospel, or he may whisper to us that integrity isn't important today.

Though we may fight these enemies, our greatest enemy could be that we don't take time to saturate ourselves with Jesus so His influence can flood through us. Nine tenths, or more, of our time is spent on the things of this world and only a minute percentage of time with Jesus. Saturation makes our walk *in Him vibrant.* When we purposely take time to *drench* ourselves in Him, our integrity surges out like a rushing springtime river.

Integrity comes when committed Christians *make themselves accountable to walk in God's Word* and *develop a strong sense of the fear of the Lord.* Then all they say, think, and do will mirror Him. The advice from Proverbs 13:6 is, "Righteousness guards the man (person) of integrity." Consequently, integrity guides and guards our lives and formulates our wisdom.

Prayer: Lord, I realize that integrity is the answer to my life, and it only comes through You and Your word. I hunger and thirst for that gushing fullness of You. Fill that hunger in me. In Jesus name, amen.

Unwise thoughts: *I've got my own form of integrity.*

Have Righteous Leaders

~~~

For lack of guidance a nation falls, but many advisers make victory sure.

—Proverbs 11:14
(Read also: Proverbs 11:10)

*R*ussia, China, Iraq, Iran, and North Korea are all countries that have something in common—leaders who have put their people in bondage to elevate their ego and their own personal selfish agenda. They are tyrants who have laughed at the phrase "human rights," and destroyed human beings with fear, torture, and terror.

Many nations of the past have fallen because of sin. The Assyrians were raised up to punish Israel and Judah because of their waywardness, and their persistence in rebellion against God. He miraculously brought them out of Egypt to have a people for Himself. The prophet Isaiah describes his unjust landscape, "Your rulers are rebels, companions of thieves." They "make unjust laws" and "issue oppressive decrees, to deprive the poor of their rights" (Isaiah 1:23, 10:1–2). When the leadership of a nation is wicked and repressive, the people are led astray or destroyed.

Fifty years later God then raised up Babylon to destroy the Assyrians because of their proud and haughty attitude. Judah's determined sinful ways made way for the Babylonians to also take them into captivity. Nation after nation has been either destroyed or plummeted because of sin. Proverbs 14:34 reminds us, "Righteousness exalts a nation, but sin is a *disgrace* to any people."

In our time, we have seen and heard of countries that have been liberated from unrighteous and wicked leaders, East Germany and the tearing down of the Berlin Wall, Romania from its dictator Ceausescu, and Afghanistan from its wicked regime are just a few. It is noticeable that, "When the righteous prosper, the city rejoices; when the wicked perish, there are shouts of joy" (Proverbs 11:10).

Will America's sinful ways determine God's judgment? For now we in America are blessed. Our history reminds us of those who sacrificed for our freedom. Some people who have always known freedom ignorantly take it for granted. The past guidance our leaders have given allowed each one of us liberty to fulfill our dreams. Nobody appreciates America so much until they go to a foreign country and observe the inequality of the rich and the poor. These people too have dreams but they can never be fulfilled.

We as believers need to pray for the leadership of America, our president, and all those he has appointed in various capacities to help our country and government operate wisely. For the lack of right guidance, our country too can fall. *Our responsibility* is to pray that our rulers may have righteous plans for us, God's plans. Not all of America's leaders know righteous principles because they don't know Jesus who desires to lead them. Most of all, those in political power need *wisdom from God.* We want righteous officials, and it is up to us to pray for them.

Prayer: Father, I want to lift up our President and others in leadership, that they would seek You for guidance and wisdom for our nation. Give us righteous leaders. Thank You. In Jesus name, amen.

Unwise action: Forgetting to pray for America's leadership.

Deceptive Wages

The wicked man earns deceptive wages, but he who sows righteousness reaps a sure reward.

—Proverbs 11:18

A Newsweek magazine had an exclusive story on the secret files of the former Iraq dictator Saddam Hussein. Some evidence that came to light indicated the corruption of his regime. For example, part of the article revealed that some members of the police force, who earned only $4 a month for catching crooks, could earn lavish *bonuses* when they imprisoned people for their thoughts and words, or neighbors would inform on each other for cash, whether the information was true or not. Members of the Baath Party hunted for traitors and were given a quota to fill. The hunt consisted of taking anyone standing around whether they were traitors or not. Each member would be financially rewarded.

In many parts of the world, a payoff *plus* your fee is required for normal things we Americans expect to receive without any extra cost: a driver's license, a government document, or access to any information one would need. Sometimes we in America have corporate corruption and bankruptcy that, when investigated, find executives receiving huge financial bonuses as their laid-off workers are denied severance packages. Occasionally we hear news that reveals individuals stealing from their employers and pocketing thousands of dollars of *unearned* cash.

Deceptive wages or money earned in a scheming or dishonest way is abhorrent in God's sight since, "The Lord detests men (people) of perverse heart" (Proverbs 11:20). Although the exterior of deceptive individuals may look so appealing in their unique or upscale clothing, God's vision drops into the very depth of their being, scouring their deceitful hearts. Scripture reminds us, "There is deceit in the hearts of those who plot evil. Be sure of this: The wicked will not go unpunished," but they will be "brought down by their own wickedness" (Proverbs 12:20, 11:21, 5).

The wise that desire God are those who sow His righteousness, not the world's deceptiveness. We are to sow His joy, His concern and His love for individuals because, "The wages of sin is death, but the *gift* of God is *eternal life* in Christ Jesus" (Romans 6:23). When individuals respond and accept Christ, they too come to know, "The prospect of the righteous is joy" (Proverbs 10:28). When once all they knew was *unrighteous* living, they now will experience Christ's Spirit and power guiding them to *righteous* living. This same Spirit will change those deceptive cravings if we *willing release them to Him in prayer*. Our longings will then *become His hearts* intentions for us.

Yes it is true, the Lord abhors deception in *any* position in life. It should not be *seen* or *heard of* in anyone who regard themselves forgiven and redeemed by the blood of Christ. You are to be a Christlike illustration to all in your present world. They need to *witness Jesus* in your life. Instead of deception, let's *sow righteousness*.

Prayer: Righteousness is what You long for in Your people, Lord. I cry out for that righteousness as well. I ask that there be no reception for deceptiveness in me. In Jesus name, amen.

Unwise actions: To excuse your deceptive ways.

The Wise Win Souls

The fruit of the righteous is a tree of life, and he who wins souls
is wise.

—Proverbs 11:30

*J*ody opened her home to a family of Kurds coming from northern
Iraq, expecting about five or six in the family. What a shocker it was
when they arrived and had seventeen children and adults with a father,
the patriarch of the family, who was 104 years old. But Jody quickly
adjusted and found other places to house some of them. She ministered
to their needs and shared Jesus with them.

Shortly after their arrival, the father had a major heart attack. He
desired to go back to his homeland to die. The doctor diagnosed that
he wouldn't live very long. Jody instead was praying for his healing
and shared this desire with his family. Three days later he walked out
of the hospital, healed by the touch of Jesus! It was an amazing testimony to everyone. Soon after, the patriarch father accepted Christ as
his Lord and Savior.

If you have won a person to Christ, you already know the joy it
brings. If you have not, I want to share one, *out of many ways*, that will
help you share Jesus.

First, find a way to begin sharing with a story, question or quotation
that is comfortable with you. One person I heard about asks this question, "Do you believe in Easter?" If they say they do, the next question

was, "What do you believe about Easter?" This opened up the way to share why Jesus died.

Second, before we can sow the seed, we have to equip ourselves with scriptures that will help people to understand the gospel story. Memorized scripture can be shared by quoting it, giving it in a summary form or even with a gospel tract. Here are a few important scriptures you will want to use:

We are *all* sinners—*Romans 3:23*; the *wages* of sin is death—*Romans 6:23*; God loved us so much He sent His Son—*John 3:15–16*; salvation does not come through our good deeds—*Ephesians 2:8–9*; no one can come to the Father *except* through Jesus—*John 14:6*; Jesus stands at our heart's door knocking—*Revelations* 3:20; we confess with our mouth—*Romans 10:9–10*.

Third, but not really last, is prayer. It prepares the heart to receive. Pray *before* you speak and *after* you share Jesus. Instead of walking past people, pray for open opportunities. Jesus taught, "Whoever acknowledges me before men, I will also acknowledge him before my Father in heaven" (Matthew 10:32).

Invite them to church. When over 14,000 people were asked, "*What* or *who* was responsible for you coming to church, or *to Jesus*," an overwhelming 75–90 percent came because a friend or relative invited them. We shuffle on in life disregarding open opportunities. Recall to memory Christ's death and give hope to the lost. Challenge yourself: the wise win souls.

Prayer: Father, give me a burden for the unsaved and boldness to speak to them about You. Help me to create a way to speak for You. In Jesus name, amen.

Unwise actions: Not sharing Jesus.

Words That Hurt or Heal

Reckless words pierce like a sword, but the tongue of the wise brings healing.

—Proverbs 12:18
(Read also: Proverbs 13:3)

I wish I had dumped you down the toilet" were caustic words of a mother to her little girl. Biting words! Expressions such as, "I hate you," "You are so dumb," "I can't stand you," "What's wrong with you? Don't you have any brains in between these ears?" not only sting but also are humiliating. They pierce the heart of the individual and cut into their very being and could even destroy them.

These phrases may be programmed in you because of your upbringing. Or you may be ignorant of this truth, "The tongue has the power of life and death" (Proverbs 18:21). James, writing his epistle, must have been observing people around him. He concludes, "With the tongue we praise our Lord and Father, and with it we curse men (people), who have been made in God's likeness" (James 3:9). You, your children, your husband and your friends have all been made in God's likeness.

James instructs us, "Everyone should be quick to listen, slow to speak, and slow to become angry, for *man's anger does not* bring about the righteous life that God desires" (James 1: 19). A reprogramming is needed in the way we think, speak, and behave so that it would "bring about the righteous life that God desires." That is impossible in ourselves—but possible when we willingly *submit* our minds and tongues to the Lordship of Jesus.

The Psalmist reminds us, "The Lord knows the thoughts of man; he knows that they are futile" (Psalm 94:11). Our wretched words result from our contemptible attitudes that lead us to degrade individuals. When we *submit all our thoughts to Christ* and ask Him to bring every idea into obedience unto Him, they will line up with His views and we will see people with *His vision*. Having His eyesight we will desire to demonstrate *His love* to others.

Keeping our tongue in check will fulfill these words; "He (she) who guards his (her) lips guards his (her) life, but he (she) who speaks rashly will come to ruin" (Proverbs 13:3). Let's determine not to be used by the *enemy* to destroy anyone. I recently heard this statement; "Control your tongue . . . God Himself can't kill words once they are spoken." We should require our tongue to bring only healing to individuals or situations. We guard our life by speaking only wholesome nourishing words. Solomon, considered the wisest man on earth, noticed, "The tongue that brings healing is a tree of life" (Proverbs 15:4).

Instead of experiencing hate, ulcers, depression, frustration and bitterness in your life, you will receive joy. The prescription wisdom encourages is that our words are to bring healing instead of hurt to those whom God has positioned in our lives. I would encourage you today to stop and tell that loved one—*I love you.*

Prayer: Holy Father, my thoughts and words to my loved ones have not been pleasing to You. Help my lips to bring words of healing. In Jesus name, amen.

Unwise actions: Destroying others with your mouth.

Are You Anxious or Happy?

An anxious heart weighs a man down, but a kind word cheers him up.

—Proverbs 12:25
(Read also: Proverbs 15:13)

A recent survey indicated, 15 million people take sedatives for various reasons. Another 35 million or more, are taking drugs and antidepressants. Why is it so many Americans require these to face another day? According to a web site on phobias, some people are fearful of the strangest obsessions: fear of laughter, falling in love, flutes, or clowns. Still some dread the unknown, waking up to a new day, their peers, attacks of viruses, and other fixations. The gloomy world news advances our fears by unhelpful repetition, which induces even more anxiety.

Webster's definition of *fear* is: an intense emotional reaction to a legitimate and present danger. *Anxiety* is: an intense emotional reaction, usually of dread to a perceived anticipated and future danger. Our times are uncertain. Business is not "as usual" anymore. We live on the edge of shocking situations happening, which enforces those "intense emotional reactions." We become overwhelmed.

People yearn for the things that money can't buy: happiness, being surrounded by family and friends, peace of mind, safety for our families, the things that make life joyful. Anxiety and fear tear down the hope of attaining these desires.

What situations are you anxious or fretful about? What can mortal man do to you? "Fear of man will prove to be a snare, but whoever trust in the Lord is kept safe," Solomon reminds us (Proverbs 29:25). Isaiah the prophet had encouraging words for the people during a difficult time in Israel's history, "For I am the Lord your God who takes hold of your right hand and says to you, *Do not fear*; I will help you" (Isaiah 41:13).

The Lord Jesus walks with you and takes your right hand too. He will not "leave us or forsake us" (Deuteronomy 31:6). Distressed thoughts do not come from Him. It comes when we get *our focus off of Jesus* and onto situations or people. The apostle Paul instructs the Philippians believers, "*Do not* be anxious about anything, but in *everything*, by prayer and petition, with thanksgiving, present your requests to God. And the *peace of God*, . . . will guard your hearts and your minds in Christ Jesus" (Philippians 4:6).

God is faithful to us even when we are faithless! Mentally deposit your cares and worries in heavens bank and *leave them* there.

With all the pessimistic news and difficult situations abounding, you really can—have a *cheerful heart*. It becomes evident when you *keep your heart and mind on Jesus and His Word*. Those pills you depend on will decline. Proverbs declares that, "A cheerful heart is good medicine" (Proverbs 17:22). A positive, joyful outlook is your precise remedy. Expressing this attitude to others requires those around you to notice the difference and desire the same. The wise will share Jesus as the only answer to anxiety and fear.

Prayer: Father, I too am fearful of all the dreadful news. I desire Your peace and joy. Help me to center my mind on You. In Jesus name, amen.

Unwise thoughts: Dwelling on the negative instead of Jesus.

Store Up the Word

The teaching of the wise is a fountain of life, turning a man from the snares of death.

—Proverbs 13:14
(Read also: Proverbs 16:20)

"Ah, man, you want us to do what?" was Karl's anguished cry as he was notified by the Christian high school Bible instructor that each one in the class was to prepare a short two-page word study on scriptures of wisdom. For Karl, studying had always been difficult. "Hey, Chris, how about working along with me on this one?" he pleaded to his friend. As they plowed into the task, they found some very interesting explanations why they should study wisdom scriptures.

As the young men cross-referenced passages of Scripture, they examined the apostle Paul's advice to the Ephesians. Becoming spiritually mature achieves that one is no longer infants in their faith to be tossed to and fro by every "wind" of teaching, Paul reminded. Instead, they were to "*grow up* in Christ who is the head of His Church" (Ephesians 4: 14,15). Karl also noticed this counsel from the apostle, "Study to shew thyself approved unto God, a workman that needeth not to be ashamed, rightly dividing the word of truth" (2 Timothy 2:15 KJV).

Karl admitted to Chris, "Yeah, that's me. I hardly read or study the Bible, so I don't really know what it says. I didn't realize there were volumes of helps that I could apply to my life." As they continued reading the apostle's advice to the Ephesians they could actually *hear* the apostle's reminder to them. He taught them, "Put off your old self, which is being corrupted by its deceitful desires, to be made new in the attitude of your minds and to put on the new self, created to be like God in true righteousness and holiness" (Ephesians 4:22–24).

"Whoa," Chris commented, "I need a whole lot of growing in the Word too. There are unhealthy desires to put off in my life that I know aren't pleasing to the Lord."

"Chris, look, here are a whole lot of thoughts on wisdom," Karl excitedly commented. "Wise men store up knowledge" and "Whoever gives heed to instruction prospers." "Here is another one too," said Chris in his eagerness. "Understanding is a fountain of life to those who have it" (Proverbs 10:14, 16:20, 22). "That's pretty pointed, isn't it?" Chris almost whispered. "How unwise I have been," he thought. He wasn't storing up knowledge, wasn't willing to be instructed, and only now realized that *understanding* would bring him a fountain of life. "How shallow I am," he reflected.

Karl recognized that he had a serious decision to make after they had completed their reports. "Chris," he said, "with God's help, I am going to delve in and study His Word. I need His wisdom to know what He is saying to me so I don't get tripped up with wrong teachings." "That is a wise decision," Chris remarked. "I think I'll join you."

Prayer: Father, I want to be wise in storing up Your Word in my heart as well. Help me as I commit to this decision today. In Jesus name, amen.

Unwise thoughts: Be unwilling to learn.

A Truthful Witness

A truthful witness does not deceive, but a false witness pours
out lies. . . . A truthful witness saves lives, but a false witness
is deceitful.

—Proverbs 14:5, 25

Jeremy was on his third DUI (driving under the influence) and was
anxious that he would lose his driver's license. Before he would let
that happen though, Jeremy was going to ask for a trial by jury, hoping
for leniency in their judgment of him. His devious reasoning was to
activate sympathy from the jurors by lining up his witnesses to testify
that he was a credible guy, and that losing his license would make an
unreasonable hardship on his family.

He then contacted his drinking buddies and his partying
neighbors and enlisted their testimony, explaining to them that he
didn't want them to perjure themselves but to "give me a good rating,
okay?" Jeremy's deceptiveness didn't work. The jury saw through these
questionable witnesses and gave him a heavy fine and the maximum
penalty he deserved.

In court we agree on oath to tell the whole truth with our hand on
the Bible—yet do we lie? Trying to get away with outright lies in court
is very risky, and people have done it. Witnesses, occasionally, may be
paid to lie; others may lie to save their own skin; and some may just
want to help the one on trial to get released from paying the penalty.
At times the truth is so twisted that it is hard to decipher what is the

"real" truth. This Bible wisdom echoes a certainty, "The Lord detests lying lips, but he delights in men (people) who are truthful" (Proverbs 12:22). Truthfulness should be a trait of every Christian.

Proverbs 19:5 also reminds us that, "A false witness will not go unpunished." This saying is incredibly true: "Oh, what tangled web we weave when in our hearts we first plan to deceive." We get entangled when we convince ourselves that we just might be able to get away with our deception. Payment for our false testimony might not come right away, but *it will come.*

Reimbursement might be experiencing guilt (including the conviction of the Holy Spirit), someone blackmailing you, or a co-worker disillusioned with your Christian testimony because of your dishonest ways. Trickery is the work of the unjust, not the redeemed believer. If you were pressured into being a witness for someone like Jeremy which of these would be said of you—a truthful witness or a false witness?

Being accountable to God wisely includes speaking only truthful words. This is extremely important to Him in any situation of our life. Jesus taught the crowd around Him that we *would be* held answerable to Him for careless words spoken (Matthew 12:36). Don't get entwined by anyone wanting to persuade you to be deceptive, on the witness stand or in other situations. *Seeking God's wisdom* and His Word will keep you actively focused and reminded that He desires truthfulness from His children.

Prayer: I know Father, that I have not been truthful like I should be. I ask forgiveness and help to make right my false words and actions. In Jesus name, amen.

Unwise actions: To be untruthful.

Hot, Hot!

A quick-tempered man does foolish things, and a crafty man
is hated.

—Proverbs 14:17
(Read also: Proverbs 14:29)

*I*t all starts like this: if little Eric throws a tantrum at eighteen months,
it looks cute and we all laugh. When he continues and is not stopped or
corrected, he realizes his tantrums give him power for what he wants.
The longer the tantrums continue without being punished or held in
check, the more control it gains on *his* life.

Now he's a teenager and it is no longer tantrums he demonstrates;
it's called a bad temper. Friends find they don't cross him or they feel
his wrath. The seriousness of this problem develops disgustingly as
he grows older. Married in his twenties, both his wife and children
are recipients of his temper, which has developed more into rage. A
person who has a temper makes foolish decisions. Proverbs 29:22
teaches, "An angry man stirs up dissension, and a hot-tempered one
commits many sins."

Quick-tempered persons are often—argumentative, quarrelsome,
causes pain and discord, and are confrontational in an overly aggressive way. Through their words and actions, they commit many sins.
In contrast, wise and patient people think twice before speaking, and
work at calming a quarrel and building relationships instead of tearing

them down. They have learned this truth that, "A gentle answer turns away wrath" (Proverbs 15:1).

Ecclesiastes, written by Solomon, gives this helpful observation, "Do not be quickly provoked in your spirit, for anger resides in the *lap of fools*" (Ecclesiastes 7:9). King David encourages this upbeat advice, "Refrain from anger (temper) and turn from wrath . . . it leads only to evil" (Psalm 37:8). "Everyone should be quick to listen, slow to speak and slow to become angry" is the apostle James' advice (James 1:19). The following scripture uniquely sums up this principle, "A fool gives full vent to his anger (or temper), but a wise man (person) keeps himself under control" (Proverbs 29:11).

You may question how you or someone you know can be liberated from the control of temper. Relying on and being open to the power of the Holy Spirit will assist *your spirit* to attain control. There is power in Jesus' name. Begin by speaking the name of Jesus when your temper rises. Your important *willingness* allows your spirit to receive cleansing as you delve into His powerful Word, which empowers you when you offer yourself to the Lordship of Jesus Christ. He then *willingly* releases the filth that the temper has built in your life.

Rage that has become ingrown doesn't go immediately. A continual submission to Jesus Christ will bring about its relief. Any time you feel yourself reacting in an ungodly manner, count to ten and speak the power of Jesus into your life.

If you have dealt with a hot temper most of your life, wouldn't you like to control it instead of it controlling you?

Prayer: Lord Jesus, I desire a gentle answer to turn away strife. I want this attitude to fill my whole being. I no longer want temper to control me. I submit this to You. In Jesus name, amen.

Unwise thoughts: Unwillingness to submit my temper to Jesus.

Discontentment Is Costly

A heart at peace gives life to the body, but envy rots the bones.

—Proverbs 14:30
(Read also: Ecclesiastes 4:4)

Unsatisfied? Discontent? That human sinful nature in us balks at being fulfilled. We no sooner get that terrific item we couldn't live without and we're longing for something else. We hear about the great bargain a friend got on a new SUV and we envy him and sulk if we can't have one too. A co-worker gets a relished job position and a great raise and it's questioned why them and not me. There's envy and jealousy among siblings, young or old, because one seems to achieve more than the other. Discontentment promotes big problems.

Moses, in the Old Testament, was a very humble man. He was given a career change from being a shepherd to a leader, when God called him to free His people out of the clutches of the Egyptians. He began to lead about three million people on their wilderness journey away from Egypt. They quickly forgot the miracles God had performed through Moses and became disgruntled, unthankful, griping and complaining followers.

Yes, some on this expedition even envied Moses. One time, over 250 of his followers challenged his leadership accusing him of elevating himself above others. Moses recognized their envy and jealousy of a position he himself hadn't even wanted to accept. It was almost comical, except it was a very serious accusation. God showed these challengers that He undeniably *had* called Moses to be their leader, and their infuriated attitude cost them their lives (Numbers 16:1–7)!

While here on earth, Jesus also encountered envious discontentment from the Pharisees, religious leaders of His day. Accusing Jesus of heresy, they devised a plan to execute Him. The Pharisees hauled Him to Pilate, a Roman governor with political power in that region. Because of the Pharisees' rage against Jesus, they used their authority and influence among the crowd of Jews to incite them to have Jesus crucified. Pilate recognized their reason and acknowledged, "It was out of envy that they handed Jesus over to him" (Matthew 27:18).

James the apostle writes to people in his day, "If you harbor bitter envy and selfish ambition in your hearts, do not boast about it. Such wisdom does not come from heaven but is earthly, unspiritual, of the devil" (James 3:14–15). That rightfully addresses our unfulfilled and dissatisfied sinful nature. Solomon calls our envious aggressiveness "meaningless, a chasing after the wind" (Ecclesiastes 4:4).

Discontentment is costly. The apostle Peter has the answer on how to handle this behavior: "Rid yourselves of all malice and all deceit . . . envy . . . of every kind" (1 Peter 2:2). Each one of us can control those restless longings. When they obsess your thoughts *direct them* to Jesus and acknowledge to Him that your attitude of jealousy, envy and greediness are not from Him. Then ask Him to change your discontentment, your outlook and your hearts desire by His Spirit.

Prayer: Father, I confess my envy, greed and jealousy of always wanting more of the meaningless things of this world. *Forgive me.* Give me Your godly contentment. In Jesus name, amen.

Unwise actions: Continue to be discontent.

Prayers of the Upright

> The Lord detests the sacrifice of the wicked, but the prayers of
> the upright pleases him.
>
> —Proverbs 15:8

*R*ules and regulations are crucial for earthly survival. Specific guidelines that were given to God's chosen people, the Israelites, after they were thrust out of Egypt where also vital. God provided religious ceremonials to Moses to help guide His people and to communicate with Him. These rites included requirements for individuals to bring a sacrifice for the covering of their sins. When the instructions for sacrifices were obediently followed, forgiveness was granted when individuals demonstrated a *humble* and *repentant* heart before God.

The prophet Isaiah records the downhill slide of the Israelites over a number of years. During Isaiah's time, many of God's people had spiritually deteriorated into participating in evil deeds and injustices. In rejecting God they had accepted idol worship, following the ungodly ways of the pagans surrounding them. Their unrepentant heart deceived them into thinking they could fool God by also continuing the spiritual law of sacrifices and offerings to Him. Such sacrifices became revolting to God. He no longer heeded their prayers.

God will not heed our prayers either, if we come with an unrepentant heart, and evil selfish desires. Proverbs 21:3 acknowledges, "To do what is right and just is more acceptable to the Lord than sacrifices." *Obeying, loving, and pleasing God* is essential for effective answers. A *fervent* prayer life is related to our *dedication* and *commitment* to God. Do you run to Him *only* when a great need comes in your life and then forsake Him with your future independent behavior? Is prayer only a ritual to you, displaying it only as a false front?

Wise individuals receive desired answers to prayers as they obey God's guidelines, accepting and *applying* them in their lives. John the beloved put it this way, "This is love for God: to obey his commands. And his commands are not burdensome" (1 John 5:3). King David was well aware of what God required. "The sacrifices of God are a broken spirit; a broken and contrite (or repentant) heart, O God, you will not despise" (Psalm 51:17).

Our selected scripture encourages, "the prayers of the upright pleases him." The Lord delights when His children desire to *wholeheartedly* and *passionately* serve Him with a humble and repentant heart. That broken and repentant heart will help guide your *everyday* decisions. His Word reminds us, "The eyes of the Lord are on the righteous and his ears are attentive to their cry" (Psalm 34:15).

A believer's genuine faith expresses itself in gratitude and love to God and His Son, Jesus Christ, in worship and prayer. These expressions ascend upward, releasing faith within us as the Holy Spirit assures that we *are accepted* and our prayers *are* heard. Precious "upright" believer, *believe now* that your prayers *are heard* and *will be answered.* His ear is attentive to your humbled and repentant heart.

Prayer: Lord, I come to You with a surrendered heart. I know You hear and desire to answer my prayers. I present them to You accepting that they are heard. In Jesus name, amen.

Unwise thoughts: I can deceive God.

Corrupted by a Bribe

A greedy man brings trouble to his family, but he who hates bribes will live.

—Proverbs 15:27
(Read also: Proverbs 16:8)

A BRIBE, it's called—a payoff, greasing the palm, corruption, greed, forfeiting trust in a key position, a judgment or conduct influenced because of tampering. A bribe is done in secret, in the dark, in "confidence." Anything that cannot be done openly, but works in the dark, or secretly, is wickedness. For these reasons, and many more, God gave wise and crucial instructions: "Do not accept a bribe, for a bribe blinds those who see and twists the words of the righteous" (Exodus 23:8).

Bribes are either money or favors given to someone in a position of trust, so that they will be influenced to do what the giver of the money or favor desires. Solomon's proverb, throws out a profound realization, "A bribe is a charm to the one who gives it; wherever he turns he succeeds" (Proverbs 17:8). Maybe it's because a fool can be bought off anytime. You might have heard this saying, "Everyone has a price," meaning everyone, for the correct amount of money or privileges, will succumb to the wishes of the giver. I hope that's not true.

A talk show hosted a roundtable discussion recently discussing the creditability and trust of government officials and those in high leadership positions. One of the speakers commented, "We need honest and non-polarized people in positions of government and leadership positions." Correctly spoken. Numerous organizations, elected officials or businesses are vying for government finances or favors for subsidizing their pet projects. They are willing to pay (bribe) whatever it takes to influence those who could do their bidding.

A bribe or favor polarizes *any* individual to withhold a fair decision needed for a particular situation. It may cause the receiver to look away while a corrupt and unfair situation transpires. A financial enticement forces people to be untruthful and deceptive. You may have lost your job because of someone who used unscrupulous influence (a bribe) with the boss. Students may shell out a ridiculous amount of money (bribe) to get a copy of the answers for a final test. You may know of crooked or devious circumstances that you could put the word "bribe" to as well.

The apostle Paul, writing to the Corinthians reminds them, "we have renounced secret and shameful ways, we do not use deception" (2 Corinthians 4:2). The believer who desires to wholeheartedly serve Christ will not be caught in the corrupt circumstances of a bribe, either accepting or giving one. God's Word is your guideline, and a consistent prayer time will direct you to make wise and just choices. That might not be the easiest decision, but satisfying the Lord is wiser than satisfying the world's ways. Don't be a fool and be bought off and corrupted by a bribe.

Prayer: Father, this corrupted world we live in does not conform to *Your* Word. I need *Your* power, *Your* Word and *Your* Spirit as a *powerful force* in me to be a testimony for You. Thank You. In Jesus name, amen.

Unwise actions: Accepting bribes.

My Plans or His Plans?

Commit to the Lord whatever you do, and your plans will succeed.

—Proverbs 16:3

As a teenager, he chose to pursue an uncomplicated future vocation, one he thought to be a respectable profession. Intrigued, I perused the exhilarating story of this young man I will call Dean. As a young teen, he thought Christianity was boring. That is, until his older brother confronted him, declaring that he was only a mediocre Christian. Then this brother challenged him. If he would let Christ be his boss and never say *no* to Him, no matter how ignorant or uniformed Dean thought He is, then he would never be bored. Dean guardedly decided to accept the challenge.

Never saying *no* to Christ brought opened opportunities for Dean to pursue communications and film directing at college. Dean arrived at this decision because God challenged him to combat some of the filth that vexed him in motion pictures. Writing Christian books, film scripts, TV shows and producing Christian children's videos, stretched him beyond his reach. He realized that once his plans and his will were out of the way, he then needed to throw himself into total reliance on God. That produced God's plans. His life has become *anything* but boring.

Solomon summarizes this thought, "In his heart a man (person) plans his course, but the Lord determines his steps" (Proverbs 16:9). You may be a lawyer, but now your goal is to be a judge. You are climbing the corporate ladder and hope to reap a CEO position in time. As an artist you are striving for artistic recognition. Release control of *your* plans into *His* hands in total reliance on Him.

Are you the one that's bored with what you're doing and your life's goals are at a standstill? Try committing yourself and your plans to the Lord each day. What do you have to lose? Yes, entrusting all to the Lord can simulate a roller coaster ride at times. That was some of Dean's experiences. He came to realize though, that any success he had was a profound realization of his own ineptness that compelled him to rely completely on Christ. Never saying *no* to Christ can be exciting, stretching, and *very* rewarding. Amazingly, He awards a calm peace that settles our inner being.

Most people don't accomplish God's purpose in life because they don't align themselves with His purpose. They now are frustrated, disgruntled and aggravated with everything they try to do, making it miserable for family and close friends. They have no real peace from Jesus. Age never makes it too late to submit your plans to Him—accept His challenge.

When you pray about your plans, then commit them to Christ, He brings your plans and perspective into accordance with His will and plans. That may seem scary to you, but it's the wisest and most significant decision you could ever choose. Never say *no* to Christ again.

Prayer: Lord Jesus, I do want Your plans in my life. Today I commit to never saying *no* to Your direction. I will respond, totally relying on You. In Jesus name, amen.

Unwise thoughts: I can't give up my plans.

Conflict in the Home

Better a dry crust with peace and quiet than a house full of feasting, with strife.

—Proverbs 17:1
(Read also: Proverbs 17:14)

*K*ids know all the answers to life. When kids ages six to ten were asked, "How will you decide who to marry?" Alan, ten, stated, "You got to find somebody who likes the same stuff. Like if you like sports, she should like it that you like sports, and she should keep the chips and dip coming." Kristen, ten, responded, "No person really decides before they grow up who they're going to marry. God decides it all way before, and you get to find out later who you're stuck with."

"How can a stranger tell if two people are married?" was another question asked. Derrick, eight, knew the answer. "You might have to guess, based on whether they seem to be yelling at the same kids." Well, unfortunately, there is a lot of yelling, arguing, and conflict in some households. Values between a husband and wife cause misunderstanding. One may believe a particular issue is important while the other doesn't.

Money is a perpetual sore in marriages. Couples may differ on where to spend their income and the way to conserve for the future. For some couples, continual limited finances cause immense pressures. Recently an article in *The Washington Post* indicated that nearly one in seven middle-income families have monthly debt payments grossing to more than 40 percent of their earnings. Another survey specified that 60 percent of divorces are over finances.

Sharing goals in balancing work and family are a necessity. With both partners working full-time jobs, and children involved in many activities, a lot of concentration is required just to keep daily schedules going. Intimacy becomes overshadowed. Tensions rise and lead to arguments among spouses and siblings. Loss of respect for one another can also cause distrust.

It is *necessary* and *beneficial* for couples to take time and considerately talk through any difficulties. An incredible amount of *giving and forgiving* is required in a marriage. Each partner would rather be on the receiving end instead of the giving end. Leaving God out of your everyday life? Put Him in daily and ask His help. Willingness to listen and each teammate praying is crucial. When you allow the Lord to help balance this struggle, you will find a settled peace in your household, resulting in many blessings for your family. Disunity in life situations can be very upsetting to children.

The advice from Proverbs is, "Starting a quarrel is like breaching a dam; so drop the matter before a dispute breaks out" (Proverbs 17:14). What does it matter if you win? Many times when you win, you really lose. Solomon instructs us, "He who loves a quarrel loves sin" (Proverbs 17:19). Ouch! When conflicts get started think of this wisdom, "A man's wisdom gives him (her) patience; it is to his (her) glory to overlook an offense" (Proverbs 19:11).

Prayer: We desire peace in our family, Father, and we desperately desire Your aid. Assist us to dissolve any quarrels and seek You for answers. In Jesus name, amen.

Unwise thoughts: I love quarrels.

His Name, a Strong Tower

The name of the Lord is a strong tower; the righteous run to it and are safe.

—Proverbs 18:10

Intriguing trendy names of individuals captivate and grab our attention. At times I think I have heard just about every name possible, and then another distinctive name begs my attention as—very original. Parents sometimes pick relatives or close friends to name their newborn after. Others pick a name just because they like it. Some names speak for themselves such, as Angel, Joy, or Faith.

Names from Bible times had unique clues to the nature or calling of individuals like Jacob—the deceiver, Peter—a rock, Abraham—father of a nation, David—beloved, Sarah—princess. These names relate to individual characteristics, spiritual relationships, or distinctive life experiences with God.

Certain names attribute great command to them: kings, queens, or presidents. Titles and names evoke thoughts of leadership, power to change historical documents, and those who influence and command nations.

To *some* the name God or the Lord Jesus Christ picture to *them* dynamic powers and abilities beyond human comprehension, which were revealed as they experienced extraordinary encounters, and remarkable answers from their prayers. The name *God Almighty* emphasizes *God's ability to handle* any *situation that confronts His people and to deal victo-*

riously and triumphantly in it. God has given all authority under Him to Jesus. "The Father loves the Son and has placed everything in his hands," the apostle John acknowledges (John 3:35). At the *triumphant, powerful, mighty, victorious* name of *Jesus* the enemy *has* to flee.

The Samaritan woman at the well was confronted with this power, and it dramatically changed her when Jesus, "one who could tell her all things," emerged. The disciples were empowered as they walked daily with Christ. King David also knew this power. He sought God Almighty for his dilemma and declared, "For you have been my refuge, a strong tower against the foe" (Psalm 61:3). A strong tower in the Old Testament was a place of protection and safety one ran to when the enemy approached. Today, Jesus can also be *your* Strong Tower.

Running into that Strong Tower doesn't mean seeking the unsaved for your problematic answers. The solution is making Jesus, who is *the answer to every situation,* your *first* choice. Wisdom for you, then, is to allow Him to *reveal Himself to you.* How? Asking God to help you develop more intimacy with the Holy Spirit avails Him to become your Counselor, Protector, or Peacemaker. These names are powerful opportunities to *grasp on to* when you need a Strong Tower at *any* given time in your chaotic life.

The world needs to know Him too as their—*Strong Tower.* Remind yourself that as He reveals His nature and character *to you, God cares about* others to know Him as their answer as well. He wants to do it through *you.*

Prayer: God Almighty, I desire You as my Strong Tower where I can run to at any time. Assist me to reveal You to others as the victorious and triumphant answer for them. In Jesus name, amen.

Unwise words: Worldly counselors and friends are my confidants.

The Blame Game

A man's own folly ruins his life, yet his heart rages against the Lord.

—Proverbs 19:3

The Washington Post added a page of The Year's Weirdest News in December 2002. Included is fugitive Harvey, age 48. A convicted sex offender and wanted in Florida, he got stuck in hip-deep snow for three nights wandering the woods of Maine while fleeing. He threatened to sue the local sheriff's deputy, who failed to track him down fast enough—a delay that resulted in Harvey losing two toes to frostbite. Harvey informed a reporter that if someone had looked for him sooner this wouldn't have happened. He refused to accept responsibility for his own actions.

If you're rushing to a meeting and a policeman pulls you over for speeding, it's not the police's fault you are late in getting there! It's your fault. If you arrive late to work every day, it's not the boss's fault when you get fired. If you can't pay your utilities, rent, or loans, because you depleted your income on sodas, munchies, video games or other unnecessary purchases, *you* need to evaluate your spending habits and not blame others for *your* dilemma.

It's effortless to fault our behavior on our lifestyle, blubbery physique, our nationality, a character flaw, family, or our past. "It was the way I was raised," or "I can't help it if I act this way (eat too much, have limited finances to live, had a dysfunctional mother, or Dad was never home)." At some time in life, you must take accountability for—**you**.

For a *believer* the *blame game* practice in their spiritual arena will create for them a destitute Christian walk, matched to their bankrupted carnal living. Excusing your spiritual shallowness by blaming people or circumstances shirks *your responsibility* for not seeking a deeper walk with Jesus.

Blame is assumed to be a reasonable justification for spiritual immaturity when it's attributed to the pastor's dissatisfying sermons or his distant attitude, another believer saying a hurtful word about you, or other illogical reasoning. We imply impossible circumstances when we purposely miss church services—"It's my only day to work around the house," or "Aunt Susie came to visit." We're deceived to excuse *our* unchristian actions at work. "You can't mix Christianity with the world's work ethics," we blindly accept.

All of these bungling *blames and excuses* are from faulty choices made in our secular and spiritual life. Proverbs states the contrast, "Every prudent man (person) acts out of knowledge, but a fool *exposes his folly*" (13:16). A prudent person demonstrates good sense, desires spiritual maturity, and is watchful of words and actions. A fool acts and speaks irrationally even to the point of blaming and raging against God when his or her own irresponsible actions are blameworthy.

Your *first* step toward *wisdom* is—forget the *blame game* and take responsibility for *your* sinful actions. Now! Confess your irate folly and ask Jesus to help you walk worthy of Him.

Prayer: Father, I hadn't realized my folly was so obnoxious before You. Forgive me. Aid me in becoming the spiritual person You desire for me to be. In Jesus name, amen.

Unwise actions: Continuing the *blame game*.

Payback

> Do not say, "I'll pay you back for this wrong!" Wait for the
> Lord, and he will deliver you.
>
> —Proverbs 20:22

*T*he headlines in the news read, "Jews on bus killed as an act of
revenge." Another headline informed, "Truck blast kills 20 in suicide
hit" in Iraq. In many nations and cultures today revenge or a payback
for a wrongful deed is an accepted practice. The retaliation is—you
harm me physically, politically, or socially, then I have the right for
revenge.

Revenge consists of: a settling of scores, to inflict harm in return
for injury. The problem with revenge is—it never ends. It's continual.
Like a chronic sore that keeps festering and never gets healed, it's always open. Revenge demonstrates only hate, bitterness and rage from
the heart, not peace or joy.

This scripture aids our understanding, "If a man pays back evil for
good, evil will never leave his house" (Proverbs 17:13), and it reveals
to us why there has been bitterness, hate and revenge in some families
for generations. My siblings and I would scrap with each other as we
grew up and my mother had this saying, "The smartest one will quit."
We sort of growled about that, but we *did* quit.

You might retort, "If we don't revenge evil for evil, we will be
considered a powerless idiot, and foolish." Actually, retaliation hits
at our human ego, and wrath controls our logic. We must retaliate,

we reason. As Christians we have available an avenue that the world dismisses. The *Word* simplifies the answer. "Do not take revenge, my friends, but leave room for God's wrath, for it is written: 'It is mine to avenge; I will repay,' says the Lord" (Romans 12:19).

We persuade ourselves that vengeance is acceptable to God. But He declares, "For my thoughts are not your thoughts, neither are your ways my ways" (Isaiah 55:8). He is concerned for every soul. Gaining them for His kingdom is of utmost importance. Revenge subtracts from this value.

The apostle Paul's wisdom is, "Do not be overcome by evil, but overcome evil with good. If your enemy is hungry, feed him; if he is thirsty, give him something to drink" (Romans 12:21, 20). Doing this baffles your rivals; they assume you will be crafty and mean like them. It causes them to wonder why you're so different, giving you an advantage to share Jesus.

The wise clue here is to leave vengeance to the Lord. How? By releasing it into His care *one day at a time*. This allows Him opportunity to replace your hate and hurts with His love. The Lord is longsuffering but there comes a time when He will not let the guilty go unpunished. King David recognized, "He will repay them for their sins and destroy them for their wickedness" (Psalm 94:23). This payback from the Lord includes nations, corporations, families or individuals. He desires to turn your situation around for His good. Allow Him that chance.

Prayer: Father, I release my revengeful thoughts and hateful desires so that I can overcome evil with good. *You* handle my hurtful situation. Thank You. In Jesus name, amen.

Unwise actions: Continue revenge.

Strength & Splendor!

The glory of young men is their strength, gray hair the splendor of the old.

—Proverbs 20:29

*Y*outh! What power, strength, abilities and dynamism they possess! Have you ever wished you could inject some of that energy into your veins? The vigor youth convey though would not be speedy enough to answer the question that was thrown out to this crowd.

A dietitian was addressing a large audience about all the materials we put into our stomach, exclaiming that much of it should have killed us years ago. Listing these food items, she challenged the crowd with this statement. "There is one thing that is the most dangerous, and we all have, or will, eat it. Can anyone tell me what food it is that causes the most grief and suffering for years after eating it?" A 75-year-old man in the back row sprang up and exclaimed, "wedding cake."

Youth culture is center stage in our society. I'm enthralled when I see young people energized for Jesus. But, does anyone want to think of getting old? We all try to delay that process with exercise, gulping health juices, erasing the wrinkles, coloring the hair or choking down vitamins. But aging is inherent. A positive attitude recognizes benefits to *all stages* of life. If the immature could identify their need and request help, those more mature that have learned some valuable lessons from their life storms, could steady their rocky boat.

In some cultures gray or white hair is a crown of respect, wisdom, honor and authority. These societies have a realization that maturity has a wealth of knowledge. My advice to those of the younger generations is this: don't shun gray hair; it has taught countless 75-year-olds wisdom along their rocky road of life. Instead, embrace it by seeking advice and counsel from godly seniors you know whose expertise relates to your need. You will find them to be more than willing to share the knowledge they have gained.

To mature adults, heed what King David learned, "I was young and now I am old, yet I have never seen the righteous forsaken" (Psalm 37:25). He realized that age did not affect God's ability to keep His own. The righteous, who have placed their lives and their families in God's hands throughout their former years, will continue to have the same assistance and protection even in their mature years. Isaiah records, "Even to your old age and gray hairs I am he . . . *who will sustain you*" (Isaiah 46:4). Keep that in focus.

Continue to bear fruit for the kingdom of God in whatever stage of life. Psalms 92 counsels us, "The *righteous will* . . . bear fruit in old age . . . proclaiming, The Lord is upright, he is my Rock" (Psalm 92:12, 14, 15). Be open to those of the younger generations that would seek you for your godly wisdom and counsel as well. Strength and splendor definitely are indispensable!

Prayer: Father, thank You for Your sustaining grace that keeps me throughout all my years. May I be open to advice from another to whom You have been a Rock in difficult times. In Jesus name, amen.

Unwise thoughts: Thinking we can do without each other.

God Is in Control

There is no wisdom, no insight, no plan that can succeed
against the Lord.

—Proverbs 21:30

Shifty aggressive plans are structured by superpowers every day in
our volatile world.

Some plans seem beneficially good, while others are alarming
and threatening. Superpowers are unaware that their designed strategies, which they view as unquestionably magnificent for their desires
to gain control, can and will be used by the Lord to materialize *His
strategic plans.*

Historical records acquaint us with nations like the powerful Roman
Empire (63 B.C.-A.D. 395). This ruthless, conquering military gained
world control with devastation, plundering, and domination. When
their successful goals were accomplished, they policed their exten-
sive domain and wisely connected their provinces by constructing an
impressive and elaborate road system. Unknowingly to the Romans,
after Christ's resurrection these roads would become the lifeline for
spreading the gospel to the then known world.

China's communistic government has controlled, imprisoned,
slaughtered and oppressed many of its own people for numerous years,
especially if they were Christians. China's tactics were restriction and
bondage, but God's plans emerged when He heard the heart cries of
the people who had been jailed, tortured, and were desperate for hope.

These individuals responded by receiving their only hope—Jesus Christ. Today, speculations concede that there are millions of Christians in China, some of whom are willing to be carriers of the gospel in their own land and other lands closed to the gospel.

God knows the evilness of mankind. He hears all their arrogant scheming behind their closed doors and secret meetings yet seemingly doesn't interfere with their decisions.

Yet *He does take from their plotting what He wants to use* to bring about His own plans. What He can't use, He will contain (Psalm 76:10 KJV).

The Lord elevates leaders, nations, and powers for His purpose, but He also processes their downfall as they become corrupt and proud (Daniel 2:21). King Nebuchadnezzar of Babylon had a dream to show him "what will happen in days to come" (Daniel 2:28). The dream entailed a dazzling, colossal statue that was astounding in appearance. The head of the statue was gold, its chest and arms were made of silver, thighs of bronze, legs of iron, and feet of partly iron and partly clay.

God gave Daniel the interpretation of that dream. King Nebuchadnezzar and his commanding superior Babylonian kingdom represented the gold head. Three more powers would rule after him, representing the bronze, silver and iron/clay. That happened when the Persian, Greek and Roman empires followed. God lifted up each powerful realm for a purpose and reduced them all to nothing as they became arrogant, prideful, and immoral.

Though the ungodly forces of the world sometimes seem victorious, God's plans will override them in the end and all evil will be brought into judgment. He will activate His plans for your circumstances too no matter how impossible it may look. Be encouraged today—*God is in control.*

Prayer: Thank You, Lord, for the encouragement of these words. I believe You *are* in control of my predicament as well. I cast my cares on You now. I pray in Jesus name, amen.

Unwise actions: Try to outwit God.

Getting Weary to Get Wealthy?

Do not wear yourself out to get rich; have the wisdom to show restraint. Cast but a glance at riches, and they are gone.

—Proverbs 23:4–5

Who Wants to Be a Millionaire? has been a popular lineup on television for a number of years. A selected few individuals are given an opportunity to be contestants on the program. The challenge is to answer the host's questions, progressing from easy to more difficult, and each correct answer increases the amount of cash they can win. Every one of these hopefuls would like to obtain the ultimate—one million dollars.

We are a society who grasps after riches. The lottery, slot machines, races and other avenues are expectantly sought after to accumulate incredible amounts of money. Desired gains are frequently lost. A survey showed that $250 a year is spent by each person who plays the lottery. They all strain for that one big break—funds that could easily meet basic needs. Others work extra hours or two jobs to gain more finances only becoming weary at the task. The prophet Haggai expresses this message from the Lord Almighty; "You earn wages, only to put them in a purse with holes in it" (1:6). Where does it all go, you wonder.

A remarkable survey conducted over a length of time found that 90 percent of lottery winners use up their winnings within ten years . . . some go through their cash in just weeks or months! Several crazed winners go on a quick spending spree and are soon in debt again. That is amazing! Great wealth doesn't bring happiness; on the contrary, it can produce a maze of problems we never knew existed.

Knowing our carnal nature, Jesus reminds us, "Do not store up for yourselves treasures on earth, where moth and rust destroy, and where thieves break in and steal. But store up for yourselves treasures in heaven. For where your treasure is, there your heart will be also" (Matthew 6:19–21).

Take note of the apostle Paul's instruction to Pastor Timothy, "Command those who are rich in this present world not to be arrogant nor to put their hope in wealth, *which is so uncertain*, but to put their hope in God. Command them to do good . . . and to be generous and willing to share. In this way they will lay up treasure for themselves" (1 Timothy 6:17–19).

Jesus confronts the distrusted Pharisees with this knowledge, "What is highly valued among men is detestable in God's sight" (Luke 16:15). Striving to gain the elusive dream drains our energy and steals our time. Getting weary striving for abundant wealth is not where our perspective and heart's focus should linger. When our focal point is to abundantly "lay up treasures in heaven," we direct ourselves *outward* to doing His work, helping those in need with our finances and time, sharing God's salvation plan or touching the brokenhearted with mercy and love.

Weary of striving for earthly wealth? Try laying up heavenly treasures.

Prayer: Father, my heart's focus and goals have not been Your heart's focus. I ask forgiveness. Help my goal to be laying up treasures in heaven. In Jesus name, amen.

Unwise actions: Getting weary chasing wealth.

Don't Envy Sinners

Do not let your heart envy sinners, but always be zealous for the fear of the Lord.

—Proverbs 23:17
(Read also: Psalm 73:2–17)

$\mathcal{I}$s it true? Do you envy sinners? You may have occasionally questioned, "How is it God allows nonbelievers to be prosperous? God sees their cunning ways doesn't He?" Maybe you know several egotistical or blatant unbelievers who display their wealth with expensive sporty cars, fantastic gigantic homes, and a prestigious job position—a stark contrast to *your* lifestyle. They acquire recognition and prominence, and people seek their presence, while you struggle unnoticeably each day just to make ends meet.

Evil ones may escape with the theft of your car, credit cards, or money, yet few are apprehended. The prosperity of the wicked rack up high living from what belongs to you and others. They seem to excel and prosper in evilness, contrasting you, who serve the Lord faithfully yet seemingly struggle for security.

Asaph, one of the Psalmist who served God faithfully, was discouraged and *also fell into this type of unwise questioning*. He described it as "My feet had almost slipped; I had nearly lost my foothold. For I envied the arrogant when I saw the prosperity of the wicked." His whole complaint, in Psalm 73:2–20, *falsely assumes* that the degenerate "have no struggles," that their bodies were "healthy and strong . . ." and ". . . free from the burdens common to man" (verses 4–5). The Psalmist frets about the seeming liberty the wicked possess. "They clothe themselves with violence. From their callous hearts comes iniquity; the evil conceits of their minds know no limits" (verses 6–8). He hears them laughingly flaunt questions to God. "How can God know? Does the Most High have knowledge?" they jeer. His alleged reasoning views the sinful as "always carefree as they increase in wealth" (verses 11–12).

Asaph expresses misled grief, "Surely in vain have I kept my heart pure; in vain have I washed my hands in innocence" (verse 13). Deceived, he wrongfully assessed his discouragement not realizing his outlook was flawed. He described it as "I had nearly lost my foothold" (verse 2). Satan, our archenemy, works in deception with us as well. Don't accept his lies. The way to escape his trickery is to follow the Psalmist's example.

He "entered the sanctuary of God; then I understood their final destiny," he exclaimed (verse 17). God's powerful presence revealed to him the tragic "final destiny" of those who laugh at and reject God. They are on "slippery ground" and would be "cast down to ruin, destroyed, completely swept away by terror!" (verses 18–19). He *finally* grasped this principle—don't envy the sinner. Their destination, unless reversed in humbleness, will be complete destruction and severance from God. Not a happy outlook!

Be passionate in seeking God's eternal rewards that *don't fade* away. God sees the *whole* picture. As you enter *your sanctuary with God,* you can receive His illumination for any of *your questions.*

Prayer: Father God, illuminate my understanding of the questions You know are on my heart as I seek You. Give me clear spiritual vision so that the enemy will not deceive me. In Jesus name, amen.

Unwise action: Receiving and believing deceptive thoughts.

Rise Up—Again

For though a righteous man falls seven times, he rises again,
but the wicked are brought down by calamity.
—Proverbs 24:16
(Read also: Proverbs 24:10)

*T*wo years after her husband died, Bonnie found herself admitted
to the hospital with an unknown illness. The delay in diagnosis found
Bonnie alarmingly declining in health. Worried, her family wondered if
their mother would survive. They solicited the opinion of other physi-
cians, experts in finding the impossible. The solution, though not easy
to uncover, was found shortly after and Bonnie was put on injections
that would start her on the way to recovery. It would be several months
before Bonnie would be fully restored. As a believer she admitted feeling
God comforting and carrying her through this testing time.

Difficulty and stressful times come to all. We feel the heart-wrenching throb of a physical tragedy, a debilitating vehicle accident, heart
bypass, the agony of a stillborn or many other severe trials. Testing
times force us into spiritual maturity. They help us to develop our
relationship in Christ.

It is easy to say you love Jesus when everything is going good. But
when you find cancer dangling in your face, it is powerful knowledge
as a believer, to know that you're not in it alone. We don't just have a
"fair weather" God who is only there when the times are good.

Someone has said that the word "testimony" has the word "test" in it. We are to allow our tests to benefit God's kingdom by sharing how God has sustained us through cancer, our teenager's rebellion, disabilities and other crises. Our scripture today teaches, "Though a righteous man (person) falls seven times, they will arise again."

The apostle Paul had numerous falls and difficult experiences. Once he was stoned and left for dead. God raised him and he daringly continued to communicate Jesus to the lost. He informed the Corinthians, "We are hard pressed on every side, but not crushed; perplexed, but not in despair; persecuted but not abandoned, struck down, but not destroyed" (2 Corinthians 4:9). *That* is a powerful testimony of our God. One Proverbs translation advises, "If you give way in the time of trouble, your strength is small" (24:10 BAS).

Calamity reduces the nonbeliever, according to our key scripture. They have no foundation to sustain them. *We have a source* the unbeliever hasn't grasped. Encouragement comes to us through the revelation the apostle Paul received in his tribulations. "My grace is sufficient for you, for my power is made perfect in weakness," the Lord assured him (2 Corinthians 12:9). We are weak; *He* is strong. Our testing is temporary, "achieving for us an eternal glory that far outweighs them all" (2 Corinthians 4:17).

As we determine to lean on God's grace, power and authority, we can acknowledge, "This too shall pass. I choose to seek Him to carry me through. I desire to mature emotionally and spiritually. I will rise up again, convinced of His excellent plan for me."

Prayer: I depend on You, Jesus. I am weak. I wait on Your power to be poured in me now. Thank You, in Jesus name, amen.

Unwise actions: Not rising up—again.

Don't Gloat

Do not gloat when your enemy falls; when he stumbles, do not let your heart rejoice, or the Lord will see and disapprove and turn his wrath away from him.

—Proverbs 24:17–18

*E*lkanah, an Old Testament Bible character, married two women, acceptable then in his culture. One wife, Hannah, was unable to bear children, but the other wife, Peninnah, had *several* sons and daughters. The customs of the day expected women to bear children, especially a son. The fact that Peninnah had born children and Hannah had not seemed to enable Peninnah a certain social power over Hannah.

Yearly sacrifices to the Lord at the temple in Shiloh were required, and entire families traveled there. These occasions were relevant times for Hannah's rival to humiliate her and gloat among the women, delighting in Hannah's bareness. On one trip Peninnah, and possibly even her children, harassed and jeered her so severely that she convulsed in tears and was unable to eat.

This time Hannah's shame was so cutting that she went into the temple and with much weeping and bitterness of soul silently poured out her heart in prayer. She made a vow to God saying, "O Lord Almighty, if you will only look upon your servant's misery and remember me and not forget your servant but give her a son, then I will give him to the Lord for all the days of his life" (1 Samuel 1:11). Within the next year

Hannah conceived and bore a son she named Samuel. This birth took away the authority and power of her accusers.

Ego loves to gloat. Rejoicing over your opponent or enemy's misfortune satisfies the jealousy, anger and old sin nature within us. We love to say, "Aha, I told you so." What you're really saying is "I was right and you were wrong," or "I'm glad that disaster happened. You deserved it. How could you be so idiotic?" We seem to revel in another person's calamities.

Why would God withhold children from Hannah and not from Peninnah? I'm sure Peninnah never considered she too could have been barren. Scripture seems to indicate that Hannah had a tender and humble heart! What control did she have over the situation that brought her tremendous shame?

Tragedy strikes your enemy; his house is enveloped in flames. What is your attitude? You are now a boss of someone who, in the past has been your agitator. You control that person's livelihood. What is your response? We often gloat with conceit and pride as these tragedies happen to those we dislike, but not to us. The Lord sees your haughty attitude and disapproves of your heart's approach.

How then are we to respond? Gloating is stopped in its tracks with this perspective; "There but for the grace of God go I." Leave the consequences of the accuser, the arrogant, the irritator or the enemy to the Lord. When He does repay them—don't gloat.

Prayer: Father, I too could be one without wisdom and understanding like my degrader. Yes, I have been arrogant when I saw their downfall. Forgive me. I purposely leave them in Your hands. In Jesus name, amen.

Unwise thoughts: Continue to ponder with malicious intent.

A Fitting Word

A word aptly spoken is like apples of gold in settings of silver.

—Proverbs 25:11
(Read also: Proverbs 16:24)

Oh, great. Just what I need—another preacher story!" were the harried thoughts of the seminary professor vacationing with his wife in Gatlinburg, Tennessee. As they waited for their breakfast in a charming little restaurant, a distinguished looking gentleman approached them after visiting with other guests. He inquired where they were from and what the man's occupation was. "Oh, you teach preachers. Well, I've got a really great story for you." With that he pulled up a chair.

"See that mountain over there?" He began pointing out the restaurant window. Not far from there a boy was born to an unwed mother. He had a hard time growing up, and every place he went, the grocery store, school, etc., he was asked the same question, "Hey boy. Who's your daddy?" That question pained him so much he avoided going into any store.

He was 12 when a new preacher came to his church. To avoid hearing *that* question the boy would sneak in and out of service. He got caught in the crowd once. At the back door the new preacher unknowingly asked, as he put his hand on his shoulder, "Son, who's your daddy?" The whole church got deathly quiet. He could feel every eye on him. Now everyone would know. The preacher sensed the tense situation. Then the Holy Spirit gave him discernment, and he replied to that scared little boy, "Wait a minute, I know who you are. I see the family resemblance now. You are a child of God." With that he patted the boy on his shoulder and said, "Boy, you've got a real inheritance. Go and claim it."

For the first time the boy smiled and walked out the door a changed person.

Whenever anyone asked, "Who's your daddy?" he would proudly reply, "I'm a child of God." With that, the notable gentleman got up, began to leave, and commented, "You know, if that new preacher hadn't told me that I was one of God's children, I probably never would have amounted to anything!"

The seminary professor and his wife were stunned. "Who was that man sitting at our table?" he asked the waitress. She grinned and said, "Everybody here knows him. He's our former governor."

A brilliant word picture is depicted in today's scripture. Exceptional positive words given at just the right time are like gold in a very expensive setting. Words like, "I know you can do whatever you set your mind to do," "You were right and I was wrong," or "I can tell you have a caring heart," can revitalize a concerned and questioning mind.

Fitting words of encouragement or healing can heap up blessings. "I accept you just the way you are," or "Honey, you are special in our eyes and with Jesus," can transform character. Proverbs 15:23 caps our whole thought. "A man (person) finds joy in giving an apt reply—and how good is a timely word!"

Prayer: Father, may I be led by the Holy Spirit to share a golden timely word today. Thank You. In Jesus name, amen.

Unwise words: Unfitting words.

Do You Have a Tomorrow?

❧

Do not boast about tomorrow, for you do not know what a day may bring forth.

—Proverbs 27:1

*B*etty is dead! No, she's alive! The ambulance rushed Betty to the hospital from the horrendous bloody accident scene. She was pronounced dead on arrival. That day had begun just like any typical day for her, awakening, getting dressed, hurrying the kids and everyone rushing out of the house to be dropped off at school or work. Alone in the car, she never saw the van careening out of control until it catapulted her across the guardrails landing her vehicle on its hood.

Betty relates in her testimony how she found herself in a blissful heavenly realm. Words spoken to her there let her know she still had work on earth to do. She needed to go back. Entering her cold, stiff body indicated life to the shocked nurses and doctors who previously had pronounced her dead! This experience changed Betty's perspective on life. The medical records she received states, she *really* did die. Now, in the morning before she even gets out of bed she thanks God for another day.

We live and plan our lives as if tomorrow will always arrive, thoughtless that another day is really a gift for each one of us. Consider—do we really have an extra day, minute or even an added second on this earth?

For some, tomorrow is the "same old, same old." Getting up in the morning we expect the same old thing we did yesterday. For several others, tomorrow may hold some very surprising and unwanted experiences they never desired to encounter. For hundreds of individuals, tomorrow may never appear. We make our plans and develop our strategies for weeks ahead and don't even consider if we will have a tomorrow.

James the apostle, challenges us to respond about tomorrow this way, "If it is the Lord's will, we will live and do this or that. As it is, you boast and brag" (James 4:15–16). We just *expect* another day. James continues to expound, "Why, you do not even know what will happen tomorrow. What is your life? You are a mist that appears for a little while and then vanishes" (James 4:14).

This is the only *real* moment you have. So live it for Jesus. Positively impact those who slander and persecute you. Assist those who are without hope. Share the love of Jesus with a hug, or a kind and encouraging word. Use your abilities and talents for Jesus today. Go on a missions trip. Communicate the salvation message without fear. Lead an unbeliever to the Lord. It could be your final opportunity. Today enjoy and show appreciation to your loved ones. Every moment of our day, life situations may change.

Opportunities to work for Jesus might be limited. We aren't guaranteed a tomorrow or even the rest of today. Do *you* have a tomorrow?

Prayer: Jesus, I realize I live as if there will always be a tomorrow. Forgive me. I want to stand before You that day and hear You say, "Well done." In Jesus name, amen.

Unwise action: Expecting a tomorrow.

The Gap

The righteous detest the dishonest; the wicked detest the upright.

—Proverbs 29:27

*I*nstalled ceiling sprinklers were recalled from a select business. They had been inserted into apartments and other dwellings built a few years ago. Sprinkler installers were contacted to pull the old ones and insert new ones. The installers were informed, at one condominium, that the lines of the sprinkler system were dry. Shutting off the controls of the system, the men began their work only to find themselves, and everything under its spout, bathed in putrid, corrosive smelling water that had stood in pipes unused.

Cunning or divisive words are spewed out, like the ceiling sprinkler, on television and radio talk shows purposely to coerce or convince believers into accepting their wicked agenda. Putrid waters can include: redefining marriage or family, questioning when life begins, the tolerating of illegal drugs, or accepting pornography.

There has always been a broad gap, a huge cleavage severing the unpolluted and the putrid, the evil and righteous, the dishonest and honest. "The righteous detest the dishonest; the wicked detest the upright," was spelled out long ago when sin entered the scene.

The line is drawn. Religious freedoms are tumbling. A person of integrity with God's values is consistently challenged in this society. Our First Amendment rights of freely expressing our Christian principles are eroding.

Righteous standards grind on individuals who embrace the debauchery of this world. They illuminate the sinfulness of man.

Some in powerful positions use conniving means to remove any religious symbols—crosses, the Ten Commandments, and others—that have guided us through the centuries. Not willing to accept God's path of righteousness some unsaved vigorously rip away at the believer's foundation stones. Infused by powers from our adversary, Satan, they are used to put his strategy into reality.

The righteous, those who have accepted Christ and are *living* for Him, will love the unrighteous with a Christlike heart, but passionately abhor their values. Their false standards undermine and snatch away the truth of God's Word. As Christians, we cannot cooperate with the world's filth and destructive plans. Jeremiah speaks of these individuals, "The word of the Lord is offensive to them; they find no pleasure in it" (Jeremiah 6:10).

The apostle Paul informs Timothy, "The time will come when men will not put up with sound doctrine. Instead, to suit their own desires, they will gather around them a great number of teachers to say what their itching ears want to hear" (2 Timothy 4:3–4). *Rejecting* God's sound guidelines is the rotten waters that continue spilling out and advancing the gap.

Greater power than the enemy is available to us, "because the one who is in you is *greater* than the one who is in the world" (1 John 4:4). *All* you need is available *in Christ*. Be willing to *invite Him* to empower your life. Your prayers are powerful against worldly corruption. With the "Greater One" in us we can combat unrighteous forces today. The gap—will be here until Christ's return.

Prayer: Greater One, I'm willing to be empowered so I can combat unrighteous forces for Your purpose. In Jesus name, amen.

Unwise acts: Embracing putrid and cunning talk.

Speak Up

Speak up for those who cannot speak for themselves, for the rights of all who are destitute.

—Proverbs 31:8
(Read also: Proverbs 31:9; 14:21,31)

*F*ive thousand homeless orphans live on the streets and *in* the sewer holes of Romania. Known as the "land of the orphans," Romania's legacy is attributed to its former ruthless dictator, Ceausescu, his wife and their government policies. In his desire to build a massive nation, he required women to have five children. Motivated by enormous greed, the dictator brought the country to poverty while his family enjoyed unlimited luxury. Women gave birth to children they couldn't care for and many turned them over to government orphanages. Today thousands of children desperately eke out an existence on the streets. Countless of them die of starvation, disease, or exposure to the brutal winters.

Shortly after Angie left a successful high-tech management position in the Silicon Valley of California, she began coordinating relief transports to an orphanage in Pitesti, Romania. Upon her first visit to this orphanage, she was stunned to realize the horrible conditions that existed. They had no heat or warm clothes in the dead of winter, and several boys had hepatitis. Beyond their physical needs being unmet, she realized that they had no one to love them. After that trip, she cried for two weeks.

Shortly following the first trip, a friend handed her an informative article in a magazine about Romanian street children, in a city called Bucharest, who actually lived in the street sewers during the winter. She felt compelled to see if this was true. Cristian, a Romanian law student, took her to this city's location one bitter cold night. Looking down into the sewer hole, she saw a girl holding a bag of glue over her mouth. She couldn't believe her eyes! As this child climbed out to meet her, twelve other children, even as young as seven and eight years old, filthy dirty and high on glue fumes, suddenly surrounded them and began to beg for food, money, and love and attention.

That night she committed in her heart to do something for the Bucharest street children. With the help of necessary aid and many volunteers, Angie started the *House of Hope Girls' Home*. She spoke out for those who could not speak for themselves.

Proverbs 29:7 shares, "The righteous care about justice for the poor." The poor can include the unborn, children used in pornography, the abused (child or adult), the poverty-stricken, and others. They have no hope, no future like you or me. *Everyone* deserves a light at the end of their tunnel. The Psalmist acknowledges, "The victim commits himself to you; *you* are the helper of the fatherless" (Psalm 10:14).

God does not require impossible things from us. He simply holds us accountable to use what means we have been given. Numerous hands of willing people are necessary in His vast field of concern. Ask yourself, What way can I speak out?

Prayer: Lord, I thank You for speaking to me through Angie's commitment. Now I ask, what way can I speak out? In Jesus name, amen.

Unwise thoughts: I have nothing to offer.

The Super Woman

A wife of noble character who can find? She is worth far more than rubies.

—Proverbs 31:10
(Read also: Proverbs 31:10–31)

*P*roverbs 31 describes the unbelievable perfect woman. To live up to her example is doubtful. Keeping up with her activities would weary anyone! Yet, there are some interesting capsules of her life that would be beneficial to recognize. Let's examine some.

"Her husband has full confidence in her and lacks nothing of value" (verse 11), displays trustworthiness. He trusts her to consider what is beneficial for him and the family. Trusting comes when our *truthful words* and *right actions* agree. It speaks of dependability. A woman demonstrates trust by faithfully implanting in her family seeds of virtue, good work ethics, persistence, discipline, respect and honor for others and God. How is your trust level with your family?

As an aggressive entrepreneur, she would be found at the flea market of today selling her wares, applying her God, given abilities from gardening, stitching garments, or fashioning beautiful clothes. I've been to many flea markets or craft shows and I am always impressed with the talents displayed. Many women *today* use their gifting in organizational ways, leadership functions, disciplining others, teaching children, or styling beautiful objects. How are you using your gifts?

The Proverbs 31 woman was also a financier, knowing that depositing, not spending, her sales profit allows her to realize her dreams for the future. Out of her earnings, she bought a vineyard, another means of income. Savers can be found hitting the sales for kids' clothes, off season items, rummage sales, discounts, or the Dollar stores. Buying off-seasonal items throughout the year eases the wallet.

Concerned for the poor and needy, she "opens her arms" in providing some of their needs from her abundant storehouse (verse 20). Today we can give to the needy in many ways, including giving new or used clothing, our time, finances or our help in food kitchens. Seeing the needy means taking our eyes off self to see the plight of other individuals. Those in need require our help.

Surveying these few thoughts, we bring *this* Proverbs 31 super woman into our century. Comparing yourself to her or anyone else *isn't really* how God regards you. He has created each one of you special, each with your own gifts, personality and beauty. *So be you!*

What does matter to God? A *dedicated, submitted,* and *willing* heart to *serve* Him determines *when you* become a Proverbs 31 super woman in *His* sight. God's delight is in one whom He can trust, who has the tenacity to stick to their given task, and who has a caring heart to serve Him right where they are. The woman who releases herself to God, allowing Him to be the Lord of her life will be graced with all the wisdom and understanding to fulfill what God intended for her. You *can be* God's Proverbs 31 super woman!

Prayer: Father, I release myself to allow You to be the Lord of my life. May Your grace endue me with wisdom and understanding to fulfill what You intended for me. In Jesus name, amen.

Unwise words: Me, a super woman?

To order additional copies of

It's
Just
COMMON-SENSE

Have your credit card ready and call:

1-877-421-READ (7323)

or please visit our web site at
www.pleasantword.com

Also available at:
www.amazon.com
and
www.barnesandnoble.com

Printed in the United States
113849LV00002B/229-399/A

9 781414 101972